Crawl Into My Story

A life in ministry

David Clark

ISBN 9798861551359

Dedication

It is with great joy that I dedicate this book to the many ministers I have known and who have poured their lives into me by just being there. Our lives have truly been blessed to have served alongside each other in the work of the kingdom. I especially want to thank Joe Cooper and the late Clark Scott as fellow servants in preaching.

I wish to thank and further dedicate this work to my children, Kelly and Paul, their spouses, James and Kate, and to our grandchildren, Jackson, Liam, Amelie and Miles. Your presence in my life is truly a blessing of God.

To Jill, my life's partner in ministry, you've have always been there and we've shared these memories and stories together. I look forward to many more stories ahead with His blessings.

David Clark
salvationprocess@gmail.com

CONTENTS

1   The Arrival   11

2   A Newbie   26

3   Friends   36

4   Help   47

5   My Happy Place   57

6   Boom!   66

7   Leadership   72

8   Phrases   84

9   Ego   95

10   The Other Side   100

11   Insert Title Here   106

12   I'm Rich   116

13   Observations   125

14   Start Crawling   132

Acknowlegments

INTRODUCTION

I'm not sure what a perfect life looks like, but I have been blessed with a pretty nice ride to this point. I have met many people, some of whom are real characters, and I have enjoyed some great life experiences. One of the joys of my life has been that as I've grown older, I have realized that I am truly blessed. Life doesn't have to be perfect to be enjoyed! Once I quit chasing what everyone else thought was important, I started to really live. I have been blessed by people who brought compassion, laughter, success, and joy to this trip.

When teaching scripture, I challenge the listener to "crawl into the story." Don't listen to scripture as a story that has nothing to do with you but rather find yourself in the narrative. Be one of the characters and learn with the emotion and intellect of someone living the event. Be Peter when you are called by Christ to leave the familiar. Live the joy of Mary and others when they find the hope of the empty tomb. Experience the fear of the lady who is caught in sin and thrown at Jesus' feet expecting condemnation — but finds forgiveness and love. Crawl into the story.

Now, with the challenge of how to read the scripture, I want to share my purpose in writing this. This is my attempt to document a few simple experiences in my life. In doing so, I challenge all who read this to sit down at your computer or pick up pen and paper and write. Write about any and all experiences that pop into your head. You'll be amazed how quickly your words flow and how you find your own life story to be. Not all stories will be humorous; your stories do not have to be enhanced. Your life, just as it's been lived, is pretty cool.

My children, Kelly and Paul, undoubtedly, without choosing to do so, gave up more than anyone so that I might preach the gospel. They have also benefited from my life by meeting and getting to know some of the finest people anyone could ever meet. They are and have been tremendous blessings in my life. To James and Kate, their spouses, I love you both. You four are wonderful and are main characters in my greatest story.

I am thrilled that one day my grandchildren will pick up this book and learn a bit more about who they are by reading about "Poppy."

To our grandchildren, Jackson, Liam, Amelie and Miles, Poppy can't put into words how much he loves you. You have brought Poppy joy I never dreamed possible.

To the reader: Thank you for taking the time to read a bit about my life. I want to sincerely invite you to "crawl into my story." I hope by doing so you smile just a little, feel alive in your own emotions and are challenged to see how precious life really is. If you are reading my story and I ever had the privilege of serving as your minister, I hope you have forgiven me for my faults and have been blessed in some small way by our paths crossing. I have loved you all ... even the ones I didn't.

CHAPTER 1

The Arrival

"Do not let what you cannot do interfere with what you can do." – John Wooden

I had finished college, walked across the stage, and two weeks later was married. I was released to change the world. Jesus had done it on his own long enough and he finally had the help he needed. Me! Humble me, fresh out of school, full of all knowledge and ready to win the world.

I sent resumes to any and all larger churches who would appreciate my talents and soon found most of them, well, were really not that interested. Looking back, a great many of them were kind to me but just not interested. Had they been, I would have failed miserably. I was high on confidence and low on ability. I was green. Carter Christian Church, a very small church in Northeast Tennessee, took a chance on a young preacher. It offered me my first opportunity in ministry and allowed me to become its preacher. On the day I met with its leaders, they offered me the pulpit. I was thrilled! The building was small and the crowd smaller, but I was ready, and I knew that this small church would soon grow to become the "new Jerusalem," the center of all Christianity.

On the way home that night, I wondered to myself what it must be like to be Jill, my new wife. She had the privilege of being married to the next Billy Graham and she must be elated. She asked, "Did they make you a salary offer?" "Yes," I chimed, "Eighty-five dollars a week!" She looked across the car at me and replied, "You sure they didn't mean a month?" As I look back now, she had heard me preach and had a much more realistic expectation of the results.

Nonetheless, the day was set, I would arrive on the scene and formally begin my ministry on December 7, 1976. If you are a history buff, that's Pearl Harbor day. Just as had been said of the United States following the attack on Pearl Harbor, I was convinced a sleeping giant had been awakened. Preacher David is awake and ready to go. Look out world!

Allow me to pause in the story for a bit. Obviously, I'm a preacher, or maybe you prefer the titles pastor, minister, priest or maybe even reverend. If you carry such a title, you'll identify with my story. Allow me one more observation. We all have a profession we are a part of. I hope, like me, you see yours as a "calling," whatever that word means to you. My reason for sharing my story is that I believe that over the past 47 years I have learned a few things, many of them the hard way. I have learned about not only surviving but thriving wherever we find ourselves. I'm not a "name it and claim it" preacher, and I definitely don't believe that if you want it bad enough, you'll accomplish it. Heck, I've wished many a time I was four inches taller and could play professional golf, but that's not going to happen! If life was that easy, I wouldn't stop there. I'd just sit on a rock and wish real hard that I could flap my arms and fly. I'd ask Jill to climb on my back and we'd fly all over the world. That's not healthy thinking.

What I do know though is that I'm where I am right now and, with a few core values in place, I can flourish. I find myself growing old and able to say as the end grows closer, "I fought a good fight, and have run a good race!" (2 Timothy 4:7) Now, back to my story.

As a graduate of Milligan College (now Milligan University), I learned quite a bit about the library. I practiced what I had learned and went to the library to study and prepare my first sermon for the folks at Carter Christian. The library is where folks went to study before computers and iPads. I sat at the table and began to read. I chose a text from the gospel of Matthew where Jesus was called in a derogatory way a "friend of sinners." I studied for hours that week; 17 pages of notes were reduced to seven. It was a long week and my first Sunday arrived. The news that I was preaching had been kept quiet. I'm sure it was out of fear that the church wasn't ready to handle the crowd my name would draw.

My morning started off in the restroom. Now, when I say that it began in the restroom I mean in the restroom sick at my stomach with nerves. To make things worse, I had hardly slept all night. With no sleep, stomach cramps and real fear, I made the drive "up the creek" to the church. Carter Christian Church, in Stoney Creek, Tennessee, was the center of the Christian world in my mind that December morning. Nearly 50 men, women and children gathered to hear their tired and slightly dehydrated young minister. I preached and was prepared for the onslaught of repentant believers that would respond. There was no response that morning.

Even though there were no public decisions, there was one very real, private realization. I had spent several years in college, studied many hours for a 20-minute sermon and it hit me. I mean it really hit me. I mean bone-chilling, anxiety-producing, nerve-wracking reality hit me. I had said all I knew to say. I was spent. Think of digging a ditch, running a marathon and swimming a mile. I was exhausted. I went home to our little apartment panicked by the thought that I must be prepared again next week. And, by the way, there was an evening service that I was expected to preach for. I'd done nothing to prepare for that. Looking back, I sometimes think being stoned like Stephen as a martyr for Christ would have been an easier calling than that first Sunday. I think Jill was proud of me, but resigning and joining a circus appealed to me that

Sunday afternoon many years ago.

For the first 22 years of my life, Sundays had been morning worship, watching the NFL, then evening worship. Not much changed when I became a preacher except that Sundays now began with stomach cramps, followed by an overwhelmingly exhaustive collapse and topped off by an evening worship service featuring a fatigued minister trying to present another sermon to a fraction of the Sunday morning crowd. To top it all off, the evening crowd was hung over from afternoon naps. If this combination was not a recipe for evangelism of the whole world, then what could be? As hard as it was for me, I can only imagine what it must have been like for those good folk hearing my simple sermons that, by nature, were short on the wisdom that life experience provided.

Let's venture out of the story again. Do you remember the first wide-eyed days of your career? Maybe you are a teacher and you entered the classroom excited -- only to have a student throw up during the morning announcements or a student curse you. Maybe you entered the business world to find your desk at the end of the hall, or you entered your first sales meeting ignorant of all the inside stories and shunned by the long timers. Maybe you're in a blue collar setting and quickly found out who the resident bully was. You remember, don't you? Maybe you are experiencing all these difficulties for the first time, or your job location has changed and you're tasting them again. Don't give up! You can succeed! I've done it and I've seen it. Don't give up!

I want you to know something about the next couple of years. Every Sunday was hard! I was learning as I went and yes, every Sunday morning began the same way – in the bathroom! And be assured, every Sunday afternoon would be labeled as afternoons of total exhaustion.

I want to share with you a few chilling statistics about the ministry. I will offer no analysis of the numbers. I simply share them.

In the Christian church, it has been found that 70% of ministers drop out before they reach their 10-year anniversary. A broad survey found that 43% percent considered leaving the ministry. I promise you that the numbers are pretty accurate across all denominations. It's simple research, but don't waste your time. Why? Because you're reading this book and we're talking about you. I want you to succeed, not dwell on negative numbers. Enough of that! Whatever ministry call you have answered, you can succeed.

What calling have you accepted? What doubts are you are facing? Here is where faith comes in. I knew in my heart that I would not stop because I knew I had been called by God to this work. It was tough and I was scared and the finances thin and ... the list goes on. I learned to trust one scripture with full confidence: "that he who began a new work in you will carry it on to completion until the day of Christ Jesus." (Philippians 1:6) There, I said his name, so I want you to promise something as you read this book. Promise that you will judge Jesus only by Jesus, not by another's opinion of Him or anything else that you have heard about those who call themselves Christians. You judge Jesus by Jesus! That's fair, isn't it?

The story continues by going back a bit in time. I had decided to enter ministry in Atlanta a few years before that first Sunday at Carter Christian. I was conned into going to Atlanta by a youth minister who was only a couple of years older than me. His name is Jim Foringer and I am thankful (now) for what he did to influence me. I was in college with my eye on becoming a lawyer. I had a hot girlfriend named Jill and I had begun the process of bird-dogging law schools.

Jim arranged for me to drive to Atlanta to help chaperone high school students at a large Christian gathering. I was stoked to go and I thought I could have some fun. I shared a room with a couple of high school juniors. The first night, I got in trouble when another way-too-young chaperone and I threw one of the students off the second floor of the building into the hotel pool. I lost my chaperone card and I was forced to go and hear the speakers.

While attending the programs, I found myself being challenged. There were two main speakers, Wayne Smith and Grady Nutt. Both are gone now, but with their senses of humor and by simply telling the story of Jesus, I was hooked. It was like I was hearing for the first time how much He loved me. Everything suddenly came together, and I knew what I needed to do. I switched colleges and majors and a couple of years later I found myself cramping, preaching, sleeping and getting ready all over again. It was tough, and I'd have to remind myself why on a regular basis, but my life had been changed.

Let's go back again to where this chapter started – at Carter Christian Church. It was too small a church to get a good preacher, and I was too young a preacher to get a good church. We formed a partnership in 1976. I came out on the good end of the deal. The men and the women of the church tolerated my poor preaching, allowed me mistake after mistake in program planning and encouraged me beyond what any person should experience. They were good to me. I still remember the laughter we shared.

I was miserable and having a blast at the same time. There are several fond memories, if not theological triumphs, I carry from those early days in the fray. I recruited some of the older teen boys and a couple of college buddies and, over the course of a few weeks, we dammed up the creek that ran behind the church. Carter Christian suddenly had a small swimming hole right out the back door. We had a bachelor party one night for the groom of one of the first weddings I officiated. We wrote notes to his bride on his back and stomach with sharpie pens and threw him in the swimming hole. His mom got capital "M" mad at all of us. We had Bible studies on Wednesdays, then fished in the creek right after church.

The October after we built the dam, small stones and the leaves of fall came washing down the stream and blocked the small holes left in the dam. That further plugging brought our swimming hole up to three or four feet deep in a couple of spots. It was an engineering marvel that rivaled that of the Tennessee Valley Authority. Later that fall, following a rainy couple of days, I got a call from a young husband who lived across the creek from the church. The dam was working so well that his yard was flooded, and water was under his trailer – and rising. His home was being threatened by a flood that I had engineered. Not an appropriate way to win friends.

Have you ever waded out in an ice cold, rain-swollen creek in the pitch dark with a rope tied around your waist and anchored to a tree to loosen a torrent? I have, all in the name of the Lord. When I broke a single rock from the center of the dam, the ensuing deluge nearly drowned me. I envied Christ's ability to walk on water that night.

I experienced my first building program at the church. We needed to pave over a small area of gravel and mud that was our parking area. It was a very small parking space and would cost a bit over $2,000 to pave; $2,000 sounded like $2 million back in 1977. We made pledges and had bean dinners to raise the money. We contracted the work and were thrilled at the improvement. It afforded a nicer welcome to visitors. Days after it was paved, a trucker turned his tractor trailer around wide in the road and crushed our new asphalt. My wife saw it happen from across the road and got a number from the door of the truck. We called and the cooperative owner paid to fix the damage. We were relieved.

Jill and I had moved into an old home that served as a parsonage. Built in the 1930s, it sat across the street from the church. The only bathroom in the home had been added years later as an improvement from an outhouse and was always very cold in the winter. I am serious when I tell you that I entered the room early one morning to take a shower and there was a thin sheet of ice on the water in the toilet. There was an electric heater that we'd turn on in the mornings to warm the room up. We were afraid to leave it on overnight because it was built into a wall corner, and I was afraid we would burn the house down.

The road that ran between the house and the church was a two-lane, state highway that literally passed 10 feet from the front door of the church. We were blessed that no one was ever killed leaving the building after a worship service in the equally old church building.

The church building in that day had no hot water. You

can look it up; the winter of 1977 was one of the coldest on record. I remember doing a couple of baptisms that year where we emptied the hot water heater at the house into a garbage can. We carried the water across the street to pour in the baptistery to knock the chill off. "If you weren't baptized in cold water I'm not really sure you're Christian," became one of the phrases we used around the church that winter.

Jill and I moved a little over two years later. It was a part-time ministry, and when I left my salary had grown to $100 a week. While there, I performed my first baptisms, weddings and funerals. I was still cramping on Sunday mornings and exhausted on Sunday afternoons, but I was beginning to think that maybe, just maybe, I could do this. Little did I know the challenges and triumphs that lay ahead.

We packed up and moved to accept my first full-time ministry. We moved to Knoxville, Tennessee, so I could be the first full-time youth minister at West Towne Christian Church. I moved into my office on a Thursday and the senior minister, Scottie Richmond, whom I had longed to work with, resigned on Sunday. Oh my! I had been there four days and had run off the senior minister!

Seriously, I worked with Scottie for 90 days and was with him when he shared the gospel to a young woman in her 20s. That night changed my ministry forever, and I adopted what Scottie shared into what I affectionately call the "stick figure" gospel. The presentation is long on scripture but easy to present and understand. I have shared that presentation with over a thousand people and have seen them come to Christ. Thank you, Scottie! I have adapted that teaching into a small booklet titled, "Salvation, A Process." Email me and I'll make sure you get one. (See "About the Author" at the end of the book for my email address).

Let me share this important tidbit with you. Find someone who is doing it right and watch them. Make it your own and use it. If it is a program or idea that you need to request, ask the person's permission. Use what you learn from others. We're all in this together, and together we can be a part of Christ's plan for the world.

Moving from Stoney Creek to Knoxville was quite a shock. We arrived in Knoxville with Jill a few months pregnant with our first child. Kelly was born in 1979 at the University of Tennessee Memorial Hospital in Knoxville. She was a gorgeous little redhead who stole my heart. Jill was a blond and I sported dark brown hair. Kelly is a redhead with brown eyes. She is a genetic marvel.

A few hours after Kelly was born, I went for the first time alone to see her. She was, as they did back then, on display in the nursery where I could admire her. Sleeping next to her in another bassinet was a newborn boy. They were the only two babies at the window. The boy's grandmother and, I assume, a great aunt walked up to admire him. I was admiring and amazed by my daughter. We were standing about four feet apart. One of the ladies looked at Kelly and said to the other, "I'm glad ours is not redheaded." Some people are not very smart! Their little boy was ugly, but I kept that to myself.

Jill and I learned one thing as new parents of a redhead. Strangers had no qualms asking about her hair. We were in a mall just before Christmas when Kelly was 7 or 8 months old. A lady walked up to us and smiled at Kelly sleeping in a stroller and asked, "Where did she get the red hair?" I looked at her and deadpanned, "My wife slept with the preacher." If the lady is still alive, she is still in shock.

I love Kelly! She is married to James and is mother to two wonderful grandsons, Jackson and Liam. I am blessed that James is also a very good friend, and I am very close to our grandsons. I love watching them play sports and grow into men.

Kelly graduated from my alma mater, Milligan University. She married a short time later and landed a job answering the phone for Fairwinds Credit Union in Orlando, Florida. Kelly is driven to do well; she rose quickly and now serves as vice president of Member Services. I am amazed and proud of all she has accomplished as a mother and a wife. She is and will always be my little girl.

I won't say more about the Knoxville ministry other

than it was a short, two-year, rewarding ministry. I met and worked with some great families and their children. They loved me and taught me a lot. Yes, like all places, there were critics, but the critics aren't the ones I'm still in contact with all these years later. Count the blessings, not the opposite! If you do that you will be blessed.

Following the Knoxville ministry, I spent nearly two years preaching at Watauga Christian Church in Watauga, TN. We grew, but it was tough time emotionally and I made the decision that I needed more education if I was to succeed. The ministry at Watauga Christian Church was followed by graduate school at East Tennessee State University in Johnson City. I began a master's program in counseling. While I was attending school, Jill was teaching in a local elementary school. I was studying, writing graduate papers and preaching weekly again in a small church. Guess where? Carter Christian Church! I was back -- nervous stomach and all. That's hard for me to believe. What is the old saying? "You can't make this stuff up!" Nearly three more years until graduation.

We grew and hosted a record attendance of over 130 when we celebrated "bring a friend" Sunday. One of the highlights of the second stay at Carter Christian was the winning of several teenagers to Christ. We celebrated 14 baptisms in one year and the church launched one man into ministry during this time. His name is Brent Nidiffer and he is still preaching today. Way to go Brent! I would leave "the creek" for good in July 1984, having served a bit over four years. We left with some of the closest friends and richest memories possible. Those memories have carried me through the rough times. Special thanks to Larry and Judy, friends who have forever encouraged Jill and me.

Someone recently asked me what I am proudest of at the end of 47 years of preaching. The answer is simple, "I never quit!" There were many hard times when I wondered if I could keep going. I owe a lot of my stamina to the men and women of Carter Christian Church. The love and encouragement of that small congregation placed me on a firm foundation for the future. They will always have a special place in my heart.

I think we should all take time on a regular basis to inventory our lives and revisit in our minds events of the past that have inspired us. I would encourage you to do that for a few minutes before you continue reading.

CHAPTER 2

A Newbie

"Take the first step in faith. You don't have to see the whole staircase, just take the first step."
— Martin Luther King Jr.

We moved to First Christian Church in Titusville, Florida, in 1984 and celebrated Kelly's fifth birthday on the beach. Life was moving fast.

One beautiful Florida day, I was riding to Playalinda. Beach on my 1100cc Kawasaki. Playalinda is an undeveloped strip of beach located in Canaveral National Seashore. I had driven to Florida by myself with plans for Jill and Kelly to come a week later. I was there when our furniture and my motorcycle arrived. I had our apartment set up to welcome them. It was a great plan.

The church staff had suggested that I take a couple of weeks to get to know the area. I would suggest that for any new ministry. They had even delayed the children's Vacation Bible School, commonly known as VBS, for several weeks until I got there. That way I could explore the area during the day and go to church in the evening to meet the adult volunteers and families. Perfect!

Back to the motorcycle ride. I had dreamed of this ride for weeks -- this Tennessee hillbilly riding across tropical Florida to the beach. The only disappointment was that I couldn't stand on the side of the road and watch myself ride by. Life was good and I was cool. Ride on!

I arrived at the beach road, a south-to-north road that began about a half mile away from launch pad B at the Kennedy Space Center. This is the pad that launched the first man to the moon. It had been refurbished for shuttle launches. It a truly historic site. I couldn't believe I was riding there. I had never imagined living in a place like this.

I continued to ride north on the road, being very careful to observe all posted speed limits and center line markings. While the road is lightly traveled, I knew this must be a highly secure area patrolled by space center security, and any type of misbehavior would be not only frowned upon but the culprit detained. I even assumed that some of the flora of the area was really space center agents in camouflage.

The parking lots are numbered in ascending order. Picture a paved parking lot on the right side of the road whose only amenity is a block outhouse with no running water. From the parking lot to the beach is a wooden walkway that crosses over the sand dunes. The dunes are covered in sea grapes and saw grass, and the walkway was four to five feet off the ground so as to not damage the dunes. There was no commercial presence whatsoever. You want a bottle of water? You carry it with you from home. Nature was on full display.

I rode north, past parking lots 1, 2, 3 and so forth. I came to parking lot 13 after about four miles. Lot 13 is the last one. While the other lots only had one or two cars, lot 13 was full. The reason was obvious. It was the last lot so I parked.

I think back at what I must have looked like, stepping off my bike, removing my helmet and casually taking a survey of the surrounding area. I'm pretty sure I looked like a rider in a motorcycle insurance commercial or maybe even like the Marlboro man -- cool and self-confident. I grabbed a water from the pack on the back of my bike and began the traverse up the wooden walkway to the high point of the dunes to grab my first view of the Atlantic Ocean. I was now a Florida resident with all the rights thereof. Employees of the space program often displayed a license plate bracket on their cars that read, "Doing What Others Only Dream." I realized that I would be living where others only vacation. I was taking it in and I was also very impressed with myself.

As I walked, I saw the head of someone coming up the walkway from the water side. He appeared to be around my age of 30. I prepared to greet my fellow Floridian. As I got closer, the shock hit me. He was carrying a beer and wearing flip-flops. Unusual? No, except for the fact that he was only wearing flip-flops. He was nude, naked, garmentless, without a stitch, wearing only a smile. I was shocked, stunned, amazed and aghast. What am I going to do? I said hello as we passed, then I looked back to see the flip side. Right there was a full moon. I had never seen this in East Tennessee and I just needed to make sure. Remember, we were at Canaveral National Seashore, home of the Kennedy Space Center. I knew he would probably be in trouble. He was, I was fully convinced, drunk.

I continued my walk over the dune to the beach. What had happened on the walkway was just the preview. I was standing on the walkway I am sure with my mouth hung open in disbelief. There were 40 or 50 people on complete and total display on the beach. All ages and sizes laying on blankets, chatting and walking. They were all naked! There were old men and women surf fishing. Believe me when I say, "That's not a bell you can unring." No, I am not making this up! They were all in the buff! They were wearing the clothes they were born in and nothing else.

I knew that the fun was over. I must take it upon myself to report this cult-like group to someone with proper authority. My mind was whirling as I thought about who to tell. I was new. I didn't know anyone. Who should this be reported to? God had brought me to Florida just in time to clean a few things up.

Then suddenly it hit me. I would share my news

with someone at Vacation Bible School. A long-term adult resident of the area. They would know who to tell. Something must be done.

I went to VBS that night. Sylvia Norton was the director that year. She and her husband Tommy would become like a big brother and sister to Jill and me. Our friendship would grow deeply over the years. But, she wasn't the one to tell. I had just met her briefly the night before. Laura Maitland would be my secretary, but we really didn't know each other. It would be uncomfortable telling her or any lady I didn't really know. Why corrupt her with such carnal knowledge? She had twin boys the same age as Kelly, but I hadn't even met them yet. The church was small, and I didn't know who I could trust with this just- discovered secret that had to be shared. I combed my brain for who to trust in this covert operation. Who could be trusted to keep it quiet until proper authorities knew?

There was a man in the church who had gone out of his way to show Jill and me around when we had traveled to Florida a few weeks earlier to look for an apartment. He and his wife housed us for those couple of days and I knew I could trust him with this sensitive information of national importance. He came to VBS that night, and his wife was teaching. Herman Wattwood was a recent retiree from the post office. He was one of the few

Titusville natives in the church. Titusville had been just a small little fishing town before the space center arrived. Herman's residency long preceded the opening of the space center. Herman would know what to do. I pulled him aside and said simply, "Herman, there is something I need to share with you in complete confidence. It is a very serious matter." He was intrigued and looked concerned. He must have wondered, "Is the new preacher a fugitive from some horrible crime?"

We went to a small room to talk. "Herman," I said, "I rode my motorcycle out to the beach today to look around." Before I could say another word Herman doubled over in laughter. You could hear him laughing all over the building I'm sure. He was laughing out of control. He finally regained his composure and said, "I guess we should have told you, but I didn't think of it. When you get to parking lot 13, the beach becomes clothing optional."

I surmised that in this context, optional meant no clothing because I hadn't seen anyone practicing the option of wearing clothes. I assume a few people might have worn sunscreen over the years but no clothing. Herman told his wife, Betty, and she just laughed. As a matter of fact, Herman told the whole church and they all found it rather a jovial matter. Herman is 92 now, still lives in Titusville, and I've had the privilege of serving his grandson Corey's family as their minister. What a grand world we live in.

A thought about the beach experience. I had Florida guests over the years ask me if I'd ever gone to the nude beach. I developed a good answer. "No," I would answer, "I don't have anything to wear."

Another observation? A nude beach can be fun if you're the only one that knows that it exists. You drive to the parking lot, tell your good friend that on the other side of the walkway is a nail barge that has run aground and formed a beautiful reef. While that statement makes no sense, they'll believe you every time. You begin the walk over the walkway then suddenly announce that you must go back to the car for your sunglasses and for them to keep going. As they walk over, you just stand back and watch. As a confession, I must tell you that I did that to my mother, my brother, several friends and a couple of gospel singers who would later visit the church.

I really do think God has a sense of humor about things like that. I guess I pray God has a sense of humor about things like that. Besides, more than a few gospel singers need to have jokes pulled on them.

If you are newbie in ministry or beginning a new ministry, I want to share a couple of things I learned from my visit to the nude beach. First, if you're going to work with people, you must admit that rarely — if ever — are you the smartest person in the room. Everybody in Titusville knew about the nude beach but me, and I thought I was the only one that knew. How stupid of me to think I had discovered something no one else knew. It is arrogant to ever think that my new snippet of knowledge is proof everyone else is ignorant of that knowledge.

Second, as I look back, I must always realize that if I'm going to be effective in helping others, I must know not just them but their surroundings. What may be silly to me is important to someone. Culture creates identity! Learn the culture where you are serving. To my knowledge, no one in the church went to the nude beach and church picnics weren't ever held there, but it was part of the culture of the town. The townspeople had learned how to coexist with a clothing-optional beach a few miles away and even to laugh about it.

Third, I don't care where you are working; this all applies. If we are going to learn to thrive where God has brought us, we must become part of where God has brought us. The scripture through the words of Paul says simply, "I have become all things to all men that I might win some." (I Corinthians 9:22). No, Paul wasn't saying become a nudist, but I will make my point with the rest of this story. Stay with me for this part.

Over the nearly 18 years I ministered in Titusville, what happened to me happened to at least two other ministers in the area. They weren't let down as easy as I was by simply being laughed at. They were encouraged to make a so-called Godly stand. They got with their buddies and began to criticize police chiefs, county officials and local city representatives, none of whom had jurisdiction over the federal beach. The local media would readily report on and stoke the battles between the newly formed "moral committee" and the "naturalists." Any newbie should make sure they have their eyes and ears wide open to what's going on around them. This will help you avoid an embarrassing start.

I got a call from a good friend and member of our church. He was the sheriff of our county. He wanted to know if he could use my office for a meeting with his staff and the naturalists. "Of course," I said. I attended the meeting, and I witnessed a man full of wisdom explain his personal concerns about the beach and, at the same time, admit that neither he nor anyone else had legal authority to do anything about the gathering. The naturalists were equally respectful and maintained that they would stay on the north end of the beach.

The sheriff listened. Christians must learn to listen no matter what we think about what is being said. Listening doesn't mean we agree, but listening sure means we care about and respect the person speaking.

I learned a lot that day about respect. Both sides were allowed to keep their public images intact, but respect won out among them. I wonder if we spent less time harping about what is wrong with others and more time getting to know them if we might win a few to better lives. It is important that we get to know people before we judge them, even if they are walking naked on the beach. I'm glad I was able to keep my reputation as a minister instead of being thrust into some space in the paper that labeled me. A label other than minister would have cost me dearly. I would have lost my ability to witness of God's love for all people.

The fourth thing I learned was a simple civics lesson. There is no law against nudity on federally controlled lands such as Canaveral National Seashore. I guess our predecessors believed that to be common sense, but as is often said, "Common sense ain't so common!"

One last, but very true observation. You can trust that this is a fact. Very few people should be allowed on a nude beach. Just as I thought I looked like a movie star on the motorcycle riding to the beach, well, I rest my case.

CHAPTER 3

Friends

"You will never be completely at home again, because part of your heart will always be elsewhere. That is the price you pay for the richness of loving and knowing people in more than one place." - Miriam Adeney

I've often thought that I would like to write a book about the many characters I have met. You have met characters too and, if you are willing to admit it, you are one of the characters that others know. You're a character in somebody's story. We all are.

I often tell friends that no matter when I die, I will die rich. Not because of any material wealth but because of the many people I have had the privilege to meet. Allow me to tell you about a couple of friends that have forever shaped my life for the good.

Jill and I had been offered the ministry in Titusville seven years before we moved there in 1984. The year was 1977, and it was a great opportunity for a 23-year-old minister. I remember driving home after that visit to Titusville. We had stayed late to see a rocket launch from Cape Kennedy as an extra treat following the formal visit. To use a space term, all systems were go for us to move to the Space Coast that year.

Jill is gifted in that she can move and succeed wherever we are, but I'm a different bird. I'm a bit of a drag on our team. I was scared to death and, on the way home, I actually counted the broken white lines on the interstate for a mile. I attempted some math in my head to figure how many "broken lines" I'd be from my familiar surroundings. (This is a textbook example of negative thinking). I couldn't pull the trigger on the move. The opportunity was grand, but fear took hold. Always hold on to the reality that "perfect love casts out fear" and that the love God has for you is perfect. (1 John 4:16)

Tuesday night after we returned home, I lift the phone off the hook. It was a yellow phone that hung on the wall in the parsonage at Carter Christian. I called the chairman of the search team in Titusville and, with a nervous quiver in my voice and full of excuses, explained why we wouldn't be moving. I hung up from that conversation with a bit of relief but a nagging disappointment in myself for my failure. I was embarrassed with myself. I spent the next seven years sometimes wondering aloud to Jill, "I wonder what it would be like if we had moved to Florida?"

Seven years later we would move. God is so good! Seven years later, I was ready.

There was one event during the short 1977 visit that would prove to be a seed of God's blessings. On that first visit of only three days, I met Clark Scott. Clark was the minister in Titusville I would have replaced in 1977.

Clark was leaving to minister at a church in Tampa and would later return to be the first minister at the Palm Bay Christian Church located about 40 minutes south of Titusville.

I didn't know it at the time, but Clark would become my minister and I would be his. We shared a vocation and a calling to preach. We would become each other's sounding board, each other's confidant and each other's encouraging brother. Clark was my hero in the ministry. He and I shared a brotherly love that went deep.

I remember the first time we got together to collaborate on a sermon series. I'm not sure whose idea it was but it was a good one. We met on Thursdays in the library in Cocoa, Florida. We had a standing reservation in one of its glass meeting rooms. The room had a study table and we would pull out our yellow pads and horribly slow, early-generation computers and we'd go to work. Ideas would flow, and deep thoughts would take place somewhere in between the fits of laughter and jest. We shared books that we were reading, challenge each other with questions and critique each other's work. While we were becoming a team in sermon preparation, we were becoming much more. We were becoming true brothers in Christ. We were becoming friends for all eternity.

Others learned about what we were doing and we were invited to speak to other preachers about team preaching. While we would have some really good thoughts on the ways and means of making it work, there was one thing that wouldn't fit on a sheet of paper. That one thing was true respect and brotherly love for the other man and his ministry. We cared about and longed for each other's success in ministry.

I am amazed at the jealousy that ministers can feel for another's success. Definitely some ministers are more talented than others, but the bottom line from scripture is simple. We are nothing more than planters and waterers; it is God that gives the growth. Praise God when we see spiritual and numerical growth in any church. Growth is a sign of God's grace and not a reason for jealousy!

Clark carried me through some tough times and I hope I was there for him when he faced hard times. I learned true friendship from him. He traveled to my home and sat with my wife and me and would simply listen during some of the darkest times in my life.

In the late 1990s I was visiting East Tennessee. Clark's wife is from this area and her mother was still living here. Her mom's health had failed and Clark called to ask if I could get one of my friends traveling with me to drive his mother-in-law's car back to Florida. She would be driving no more. "No problem," I said, and the next day I picked up the car for the drive back.

I moved back to East Tennessee to minister just a few months later. I was meeting with my staff at the church one day when a police officer walked in. I spoke up rapidly and joked, "I hope you're not here to arrest me." He said, rather dryly, "I need to talk to David Clark." I admitted my name and we went to my office. It seems that Clark's mother-in-law, whose health and mind were slipping, had called police and reported her car stolen. She told them that David Clark, the new minister at Boones Creek Christian Church in Johnson City, Tennessee, had stolen it. A couple of phone calls cleared everything up but Clark loved it!

Clark passed away from a chronic illness not long after I moved here. I spoke at a memorial service held for him at his burial. I miss you, Clark, and look forward to our reunion one day.

Carl and his wife attended our church in Titusville on a regular basis. That is, if you count Easter, Mother's Day, Father's Day and the candlelight Christmas service as regular. They did so to please his mom and dad. When they entered the church, they looked like Barbie and Ken. They carried the air of young, good looking and very successful. She was pretty and he handsome and very successful at an early age. To be honest, they bothered me a little. I felt like he thought he was gracing us with his presence. I loved his mom and dad and kept my thoughts to myself.

Carl's dad came to my office one day in 1986 and asked if I would go talk to Carl. He was at his parent's house and was dealing with emotional stresses and facing hard decisions. I didn't want to go, but I did. I went after lunch one Saturday when only Carl was there.

He greeted me at the door. I didn't expect what I saw. He was in shambles! He was barefoot, in an old pair of jeans and a simple white t-shirt. His personal appearance was haggard. We went in a small den and began to talk. He was broken and I must admit that I learned I was broken, too. I had made rash judgements that no Christian should make, and I was a minister.

I listened with no immediate answers; I was not hearing words that made sense but rather words that came from deep pain -- words used when one is deep in the grip of fear, facing their own failures and anxiety. The words themselves don't always make sense, but if you listen not only to what is being spoken but how it's being expressed, you begin to see a picture of reality. I was listening to a man who was broken.

Carl was burdened by the weight of his personal failures in life. We all face personal failures and they hurt deeply. We may be victims of failure or, as is most often the case, we have brought it on ourselves. We face our sins, and the pain is deep and leaves wounds that won't heal on their own. He was in trouble and being honest, and I was being exposed. Exposed for my own arrogance, my damnable attitude of judgement and my "better than you" feeling of self-righteousness. Remember, it was 1986.

Flash forward 12 years to July 1998. It was one of the biggest and most distinguished crowds I had ever spoken in front of. The city council was all in attendance. The county sheriff and at least five police chiefs were there along with representatives from the governor and congressional offices. All the elected officials from the county were sitting with Carl's family near the front of the church. We were in a large church that held over 1,200 people and it was beyond capacity. My dear friend Carl had passed.

He had, by this time, become the police chief in Titusville. The damnable disease of cancer had taken my friend and we were there to remember his life. Carl left a legacy of fairness and community encouragement. He had given countless hours to coaching youth in sports, and he was active in civic clubs. He was a mentor in the Big Brother program.

Without citing more accolades, he was one of the most loved public officials anyone would ever know. His funeral processional would stretch over three miles and his graveside would feature a color guard and a flyover. What would I say?

Following the speeches of some local officials, I stood. My heart was breaking. I shared a couple of stories about my best friend. He was my fishing buddy and, like me, father to a daughter and a son. His wife was a good friend of mine and my wife a good friend of his. Our families camped together in the Florida Keys. He and I traveled to the mountains of East Tennessee several times to stay in a cabin on Watauga Lake. We rode bikes together five days a week, played scores of softball games and spoke daily. Carl was a best friend. We were like brothers, laughing and sharing life for far too short a time. More than anything he was a Christian brother. I know, as I shared with that crowd that day, that Carl's cancer won a battle that July 19, but I know that Carl's faith won the war. I truly look forward to seeing him again. To this day though I miss him.

I often am reminded of how my self-righteous attitude almost cost me this important relationship! Jesus said that we shouldn't judge others and I wasn't listening years earlier when I was guilty of judging Carl. His dad forced me to meet him, to sit and talk, and I am forever grateful that I did.

Don't ever take for granted the blessings of friends. Embrace every opportunity you have to spend with others and learn to be excited at their presence. The people you spend time with will challenge you and make your life better. Listen to what they say and what they laugh about. Learn to appreciate the things that make them cry and move them to action. I shared that day that Carl had embraced living life and, in doing so, had brought energy and hope to others. I hope I spoke a few words of comfort to his wife Kathy and children Jenny and Brian. I know he loved them deeply. I pray his mother and father, who adored him, left that day with hope. And to his sister, I pray there was encouragement.

Someone told me at the time of Carl's death that few people will ever really have a best friend. That observation encouraged me to always be thankful that I did. I wasn't Carl's only close friend, nor he mine, but we truly did share a closeness as friends that is rare and a gift from God. I miss you Carl and look forward to our reunion one day.

Please don't ever miss out on the chances God gives you to know people. I've met and been allowed to know a lot of people. I've learned a lot from all of them and, in the process, been able to understand myself a bit better. Most everyone I've known has helped to shape me in a positive way and has made my life richer. Allow me this observation too. There are a few I wished I'd never met! I bet that sounds familiar. Do you want to thrive in life? Embrace the friends you have. Seek to build them up and thank God for them daily.

Jesus said, "Greater love has no man than to lay down his life for a friend."(John 15:13). Jesus did that for us and I hope it can be said that I have done that too. I know I can do a better job. I'm glad I knew Clark and Carl, and I praise God daily for what our short years together taught me about friendship. Friendship doesn't end at the grave because it lives in the heart. Don't ever forget that!

It seems that every message we receive is communicating that we should accomplish all that we can accomplish and grab all that we can grab. I'm going to tell you a truth after nearly 50 years in ministry. Outside of my relationship with God, my wife and kids, the most important gift I have ever received is the gift of a great many friends in my life. I grew up having lost my father at an early age and without much at all to show in the way of things. Friends are my wealth and wow, am I ever wealthy! I bet you are wealthy too.

I hope by sharing this glimpse of my relationship with my deceased friends you'll do an inventory of your friends. I've had a lot of great friends and many stories I could tell. They have influenced me more than they will ever know.

Please allow the two stories I've told to make a big impact on your thinking. Whatever your current place in life I encourage you to do something very important. Make a list of your friends and your memories. I promise it will lift your spirits and, no matter where you are, will help you to grow in life. Do it!

One last footnote to the stories of Clark and Carl. They became close friends! Before Carl left the sheriff's department to become city chief he had advanced to rank of commander. Carl introduced me to then-sheriff Jake Miller. Jake began to attend our church and approached me one day to see if we could develop a chaplaincy program for the Brevard County Sheriff's Department. I didn't know what it would take but asked if Clark could be a part of the program. With the sheriff's approval and offer of some training we launched the program. Clark was on the south end of the county and I was on the north end. Clark stepped down a few years later for health reasons and I stepped aside to become a chaplain with the city. What sweet the memories of Clark and Carl, my two great friends.

Let me repeat: Take inventory of your friends right now. Is there anyone you need to call?

Help

"Help me if you can I'm feeling down and I do appreciate you being round."
-John Lennon/Paul McCartney

Hello. My name is David and I have a problem. Will you help me?" The group answers, in unison, "Hello David. Yes, we will help you." The truth of the matter is, I didn't have a problem! Everybody else in the room did, but I didn't. I was surrounded by alcoholics, pill poppers, crackheads and junkies. They knew everything about pot, pills and powder, and I knew nothing.

I have never drank alcohol, done drugs or eaten coleslaw. Never! I was fortunate because my dad had the talk dads are supposed to have with their sons about drugs. He said simply, "If I ever catch you doing drugs, I will kill you." As to alcohol, it was never in our home and the same rule applied. My dad had been raised as an adamant teetotaler.

Alcohol nearly killed my grandfather when he was young so we weren't exposed. In his youth, he endured and came close to death due to a condition called jake leg. Symptoms were partial paralysis of the feet and legs caused by drinking improperly distilled or contaminated liquor. My Poppy made a vow to God from his almost-death bed. He kept his vow.

As to coleslaw, just like beer, it tastes awful. So, I was never exposed to drugs and there I sat in a roomful of addicts asking them to help me.

I don't know how it happened. I don't even remember who the first person was, but my ministry in Florida found fertile soil among drug addicts. They would come to church to worship and then, in a couple of weeks, they would tell me of their addiction. You name it. Pot, smack, and the worst at the time, crack, and a life is ruined. There were those who were attached to legal drugs. Substances like alcohol, pain pills and muscle relaxers created people who were willing to steal, lie, destroy relationships and bankrupt families simply to get the fix. In my mind, I must admit, the first problem they had was that they were stupid.

Over a few short years, I saw some hard things — a young man lying dead across a car seat with his eyes wide open and face frozen in terror (more about him in Chapter 11). I was with the sheriff's department as a chaplain at the retrieval of three bodies from a ditch. They had been murdered and set on fire in a drug deal gone badly. I met and became friends with an addict who, in a crazed state, ran from police and hit a family in a Jeep head on. His behavior sent a 4 year old to the hospital. He nearly killed himself and he's maimed for life.

I had a childhood friend move to the Titusville area. He lost his son in a set-up robbery designed to steal a gold necklace to sell for drugs. The young man had an emotional attachment to the necklace and fought to keep it. He was killed by a friend who was desperate for drugs.

Another vivid memory is of a 12-year-old boy laying across his dad's chest in a hospital crying out, "Why daddy? Why daddy?" His dad, in a drugged craze, argued with the boy's mother and shot himself. I escorted the young son for what was to be his last visit before life support was withdrawn. I preached at his funeral.

I asked myself over and over and over, "How could someone be so stupid? Why, why, why do they think it will not do to them what it has done to everyone else? How can a person be so stupid?"

"Hello. My name is David. I have a problem and I need your help. Will you help me?" What brought me to this point? It was simple. I was sitting next to a young man in his twenties I had promised I would accompany if he would get help. I felt imposed upon at this point. They all thought I was an addict. "I'm not like you!" I wanted to scream. But I couldn't say, "Hello. My name is David and I have NO problems." No problems. That would be an awfully big statement, so I went along. I listened that night.

In the group were professionals, men, women, blue collar workers, college students, married couples and singles -- all bound together by a plague from the front porch of hell. Addiction! They had lost their marriages, their children, their homes and their jobs. They told stories of rejection, crime and loss of identity. All the stories had the same ending. They slept in their cars, in tents and a few under the stars. They had hit the proverbial bottom and had nowhere to turn. Yet, understanding fully the literal bondage in which they were living and wanting release, more would fail than would succeed. "Why were you so stupid to begin with?" I wanted to ask.

Years later, a new friend named Ben called and asked if I would teach the Bible to a group of men for one hour a week. "Sure," I said, "What do you want me to teach?"

Ben had joined with his best friend and his friend's wife to start a program to help men recover from addiction. They came from all over the country to East Tennessee to attempt recovery in a faith-based program. Ben answered my question as to what to teach -- "Share the scripture and your heart." I was older and determined to do just that. Teetotaler teaches addicts. God has a sense of humor.

One of the first times there I told the addicts how I felt and asked the question, "Why? Why did you think you could be the one that could cheat and not end up

addicted? Why the first time?" They began to answer.
Boy, did they ever answer and, in the midst of my
confusion, I was brought down and humbled by what I
heard.

One told me of his first use of drugs at age 18; another
told me of being introduced by a family member at age
15. Now, the convicting truth of what I heard -- every
other man sitting there (one was in his 50s) had been
introduced to the chains of hell between the ages of 10
and 14. You know what really left me moved and aghast?
I found out real quick who introduced them.

One man had stolen a beer from his father's stash and
drank it at age 13. He got a bit of a buzz and bragged about
it to a friend. He and his friend then did that together and
felt like they were grown up. They got together with five
or six other school mates to repeat the experiment, and
one of the friends brought an even older friend. The older
boy stuck a needle in this young man's arm while he was
under the influence. He was 13 years old and now using
meth. You and I can only imagine the next 15 years for this
young man. I hope you can only imagine.

I heard stories of mothers and fathers sharing alcohol
and drugs with these youngsters. I heard about older
brothers and sisters giving pills to them and their friends.
I learned about the pain of divorce and the feeling of
rejection at an early age and how the one with the drugs
would make them feel welcomed and accepted. They told

me about prescriptions they were exposed to by mom and stocked cabinets that dad seemed to worship.

Were they stupid? No! They were kids! Innocent, naive and wanting to fit in. They were willing as children to do anything to fit in anywhere, and their lives had been left in drug-induced addictions. Five, 10, 15 and 30 years later, they are unable to function outside of the influence. Most were addicts since childhood. The most mature had been addicts since high school. I learned they weren't stupid but so often victims of some of the most damning of sins — the abuse of children. They were alone in their struggles to survive.

I guess you've figured out by now who was the stupid person in the room. I have learned a lot through this journey with addicts. We all have problems and we all need help!

Being the sober one among the addicts taught me a lot. I'm not even sure as I write this if I'm able to put into words what was revealed to me. I do suspect that if you've read this far you've had your life impacted by or have at least witnessed the scourge alcohol and drug abuse can bring. Please I ask, as I share some of what I have learned, don't read what I'm going to share as clichés to be skipped over.

Clichés are only clichés if they aren't from the heart, and what I'm going to share is, if nothing else, from the heart. Here's what I've learned.

First, I learned that I do need help. You know what is the main difference between me and a drug addict? Their problem is on full lit-up-like-a-carnival display and my problems aren't. I can be living scared to death, full of anger, in lust or addicted to greed and get up every morning, shower and get dressed, and you'd never know I had a problem by looking at me. If you are a person of honesty you'll understand firsthand the truth spoken in the scripture when it says, "All are sinners and have fallen short of the glory of God."(Romans 3:23) I don't care how good you appear, you'll be better in life if you admit that.

I won't be sleeping in my car, losing my teeth and suffering from malnourishment but, I will still be dying. When life is being sucked out of your soul — it doesn't matter if it by alcohol or greed, heroin or lust, opioids or anger, Xanax or gossip, meth or bitterness — you are still dying. Just like the addict we can be dying on the inside and want so badly for things to be different. But they aren't. I often need help so that I don't keep living day in and day out the same old way.

Second, I've learned that to ask for help means we must admit we are weak. For reasons bigger than ourselves, we don't want to own weakness. We think that to admit weakness must mean we are weak. Jesus said that, "Satan is a liar and his native tongue is lying." (John 8:44) We live his lie when we exist day after day after day always afraid to say, "I am weak." I bet you've known people who you'd never want to know that you were struggling. Well guess what? They are struggling, too. Admitting we are weak and need help is an act of strength.

Listen, I've heard folks who are addicts talk trash about other addicts as if they aren't one. One of the most common refrains of an addict is, "I can quit anytime I want to." Over and over all they say is, "I'm not weak and I'll never admit that I need help." I learned sitting in the group and being forced to say, "I need help. Will you help me?" that I have personal struggles. I learned that, on my own, I am weak!

Third, I have learned that there is always an excuse for delaying the help that is needed. A very common refrain in the world of drugs is "I'll get help right after ..." You fill in the blank. When a boat is taking on water you'll never hear the captain say, "We'll fix the breach right after the next cruise." Addicts will often say something along these lines. "I can't get help now. I have kids I've got to take care of." They've robbed from their spouses, been in jail and aren't allowed back home and they'll say, "I must help the kids." What excuses are you using to delay accepting the help you need in your life?

Fourth, I've learned that some people will never care about anyone else and will even rejoice in other folk's failures. Those who relish in and talk about other's failures are held in the worst of bondage. It's like a little kid who finds another kid covered in more mud than he is and decides, "Since they are dirtier than me I must be clean."

I couldn't believe the actions of one mother who came to her son's graduation from a rehab program. After years of addiction, he had been clean for a year. He was going home with his parents. She belittled him at graduation and told him repeatedly that, "He now thought himself better than her." She was an addict and couldn't stand that her son was clean. He had to walk away from her until she got help. Praise God she later accepted help.

I must admit that, embarrassingly, I hear that attitude a lot among Christians, Christians who like to preach and sit in judgment of others who are hurting. So often we find ourselves critiquing others by thinking them stupid. Ouch! Remember, one of the biggest warnings ever spoken by Christ was "Judge not." (Matthew 7:1)

Lastly, I have learned that there is help — no matter what the need. Yes, sometimes it's hard to find and there may be some counterfeit help floating around, but there is help. I learned from recovered addicts about counterfeit help. Let me give you one example. I am only relating what I was told. They spoke to me about prescribed drugs designed to aid one in leaving an illegal drug. One addict told me that all he was doing was switching addictions. Another said it this way, "I could buy an illegal drug on the street corner or a legal drug in the building on the corner. Either way I was still addicted." Please listen.

I know you're probably not a drug or alcohol addict, but is there something you need help with? Don't settle for counterfeit help. Real help is available.

I know of a place you can find help right now — no matter what the need. But first, I want to ask a favor of you, just as I did earlier. Will you please judge Jesus by Jesus and not by those of us who are, at best, struggling daily to follow him? He said simply, "Come to me all who labor and are heavy laden and I will give you rest." (Matthew 11:28) Are you tired? Somebody near you is ready to help. They may not know it yet, but the hope of Christ is living in them and they will help you find that rest.

When I was forced to say, "Hi, my name is David and I have a problem. Will you help me?" it surprised me how the plea spoke to me and has helped me navigate life. I hope such an admission of need will help you too. I've never used drugs or alcohol, but I found help among the addicts!

CHAPTER 5

My Happy Place

"There is no other condition and no other place where you will be as happy as the place of your calling."
– Sunday Adelaja

It was fairly early in the morning, around 9 a.m., and I was in my office reading. An active member and leader of the church named Herman came by and, after chatting for a few minutes, asked what plans I had for the day. I told him I was going to make a couple of visits to some folks from the church and then have lunch. Following lunch, I was going south of Cocoa to pick up some furniture. A family in the church built and sold various styles and colors of patio and beach furniture and had called to donate some to our nursery. We were beginning to attract some younger families, and this would be a big help.

"Do you mind if I go with you?" he asked. "Of course not," I answered. "If you've the time, let's go." We headed out merrily on our way. Our visits were good and, as always, took a little more time than anticipated. We picked up a third on the way to lunch and didn't get to

Cocoa until midafternoon. We visited there a bit and then headed back to the church.

We were carrying the furniture in a back door and I set a piece down and went to visit the restroom. Keep in mind this is a small church and we had two single-person restrooms. I was in the rest room when Herman pecked on the door and said sheepishly, "David?" I wondered what could be so important that it couldn't wait for one or two minutes. "David?" "What Herman?" He then asked, "Did you turn the water on in the baptistery?"

A baptistery, if you aren't familiar, is a pool built inside a church designed to hold enough water for two adults to stand in waist deep. The purpose is so that one person can baptize the other. This takes place when the baptizer (most often the preacher) leans the person being baptized back into the water, submerging them and then lifting them forward so they are again standing.

This ceremony is very important and solemn. A person has, in faith, accepted that they are a sinner in need of a savior. Because of that desire they will stand in the water as a sinner, ceremoniously die and be buried under the water, and then in imitation of Christ's death and resurrection stand up representing the birth of a new person. It is a very spiritual ceremony. If you want more information please read about it in Romans 6:3-7. Interestingly enough, the Bible explains it much better than I.

Most baptisteries are built into the architecture of the church almost always in the front wall so that the baptism can be witnessed by others. The original church building in Titusville was different. The man who built the church normally built houses, and he didn't know what a baptistery was when they told him what they wanted.

The baptistery pool wasn't purchased; it was constructed out of block and then lined like a pool. It had steps leading down into it. It was originally nearly 10 feet deep so that if a couple of people went into it they couldn't be seen. Consequently, the men of the church had added an extension to the drainpipe — raising it up until it was about three and a half feet deep to the bottom — and poured lots of concrete to fill it to the top of the pipe. It was filled by a simple spigot with a piece of hose attached. No emergency drain whatsoever. Are you ahead of me?

"Yes Herman, I filled the baptistery." I had turned the water on that morning about 8 a.m. to simply raise the water up a couple of inches in anticipation of a couple of baptisms on Sunday. The water had been running for nine hours or so. When I say running, I mean over the front wall of the baptistery, onto the auditorium stage and the main floor soaking all the carpet, all the flooring and furniture and -- are you ready for this? – running out the front door. I had flooded the place. I had performed a miniature reenactment of Noah's great flood.

Small objects were floating.

Herman went to the room where people changed for a baptism and brought out a garbage can and several towels. I kid you not when I say that to soak all the water up with towels, wring them out, then dump the water would take somewhere in the neighborhood of a year. Desperation set in.

Jill and I had planned to host dinner that night with four or five new young couples who had been visiting the church. After dinner, we were all going bowling. I called to cancel and everyone of the invited people said they would come help.

We rented several wet vacuums from U-Haul. We set up large, rented fans and left the windows open overnight. It was way past midnight when we left. We repeated the process on Saturday. We had church on Sunday and had the cleanest carpet imaginable. It was still damp in places but not soaked. Now, I will tell you, without going into detail, that I did the same thing about three weeks later. Yes, I did! Some of us learn more slowly than others. This time, it smelled a bit underneath the stage. We had to pull the carpet up from the front of the stage and allow the area to dry out for a week, put it back for church, and then lift it up again. I'm sure it was a lot simpler when the church used to gather at the river for baptisms. I sure know it is easier when a baptistery pool is purchased to be a baptistery pool and built into the church with an overflow drain.

About five weeks after the first time I flooded the building we were sitting in church and, during communion, the most solemn part of the worship service, a man named Wayne started whispering from the back row of the choir. In an ever-increasing volume he was calling, "David, David, David!" I finally heard him and made eye contact. He pointed to the wall behind him and whispered pretty loudly, "Water!" Water was running over the wall from behind the choir and pooling around Wayne's feet. I had done it a third time.

One of my best friends ever, Tommy Norton, started checking the baptistery every week to make sure it was filled to the correct depth. I wasn't allowed to touch it again!

I titled this chapter "My Happy Place." Here is why. I love the baptistery in a church because I believe it is a place where we see Heaven connect with earth, where God connects with man and where lives are changed in a moment. It is the culmination of a person owning their foibles, their failures, their sins and, in a very tangible way, accepting the loving forgiveness God offers and beginning anew. When one does this in faith, our faith tells us that they receive the help of God living in them. That life in them is called the Holy Spirit and this is explained in the Bible in the book of Acts Chapter 2, verse 38. Read it if you never have.

Now, one more event in the demon-possessed baptistery of that church. It drained through piping under the building into the sandy soil of Florida. Water retention at its best. The church had a well and we put the water right back into the ground. There was one problem. When we had grown to the point that we would need to build a new worship area, we would need to cover up the outside valve that opened the drain. We had a problem that needed to be solved.

Tommy and I engineered a solution. We opened the drain permanently. We designed a simple solution. We took a piece of plastic pipe and fitted it into the drain in the baptistery with an O-ring around it. Yes, the water leaked out slowly but slow enough that Tommy could come in and top it off on Saturday in anticipation of baptisms on Sunday. It added the extra luxury of providing an emergency overflow should the water get too high. The pipe was cut to stand about two inches above a comfortable level. Brilliant, simply brilliant!

On the first Sunday after our new engineering project, a lady who had moved to Florida from Michigan voiced her desire to be baptized. I was thrilled, the church was thrilled, and she was thrilled. We readied after the service for the baptism and almost every person stayed to encourage and welcome her to her new life. She and I changed, and I came to the pool from the right side and waited on her to enter. She came from the dressing room wearing a white robe, me in waders with a robe over them.

There is an opening in the wall framed with a curtain hanging in front of it. Once we were in the water, Herman would pull the strings on the curtain rod and the curtains would open to reveal us in the water. Herman stood on one side and his wife on the other to welcome her after the baptism. The curtain opened and the congregation waited in anticipation. They always sang "Now I belong to Jesus" when the person was lifted out of the water.

Tommy and I had designed the baptistery drain with a small cork plug on the top to handle the rise of the water when a couple of folks entered the pool. Cork, how stupid. We stood in the water and I began to speak. I introduced the lady and then I began to pray. While praying the cork came loose from the pipe and water began to go down the pipe. Keep in mind we were standing in a pool with walls around it on three sides and an opening in the fourth wall for witnessing the baptism. The design of the room made it a natural sound amplifier.

I bet you've never heard an elephant passing gas in a pond have you? Well I have! At least, I think that is what it would sound like. The water going in that pipe made the most unchurch-like sound I have ever heard. Cup your lips against your arms and blow out. That is the sound it made and there we stood.

In a panic, I reached back and placed my hand over the drain. I looked to my left with a "please help me" look to Herman and he was folded over laughing. The congregation was laughing. There we stood, unable to move without creating a sound like no other. After a few seconds, I grabbed the pipe, pulled it out of the bottom of the pool, allowed the water to start draining from the bottom and, as it was doing so, baptized the lady. Herman closed the curtain with tears running down his face. The Bible records a time when 3,000-plus people were baptized in a day. I bet not a single one was as memorable as this one. The lady remained with the church as an active Christian until her move. God for sure has a sense of humor.

My happy place is the baptistery because, as I said, I am not just an eyewitness but a participant in God reaching down to touch man. It is a grand thing to be part of and one that words can't describe.

A few years later, in a new building with a state-of-the-art baptistery, I stood waiting in the pool for a man named Greg. Greg came to worship with his wife Tyka and his two younger brothers. He and his teenage brothers had all made the decision to be baptized. It was a grand day and the packed church watched with celebration and joy. The youngest brother first, then the next, and then it was Greg's turn.

I turned to Greg and quietly said, "Make sure to use

the handrail as you come down. It's easy to slip." I stood
at the bottom of the steps facing him. Greg, who was in
his mid- 20s, smiled and started down the steps without
taking hold of the rail. He slipped on the top step and his
feet flew forward. He hit all four steps on his way down
with four loud aquatic thumps that resonated throughout
the building and then took my feet out from under me.
He and I both went under.

I always wore waders. Waders, if you aren't familiar, are
waterproof pants that go up to your chest and are held up
by suspenders. I wore them in the baptistery over my suit
pants and dress shirt. Well, the waders filled with water
and I quickly gained about 40 pounds of extra weight.

Greg and I stood up, soaked with our hair down
over our foreheads and water dripping off our chins.
I baptized him without saying a word because I was
about to explode into laughter. I could hear his brothers
laughing just out of sight to my right. Greg sheepishly
stepped out of the baptistery. I looked very seriously at
the congregation, who were sitting stone silent, and said
loudly as I pointed to them, "Don't anybody tell me Greg
hasn't been baptized." They roared with laughter. I had to
speak loudly because we had destroyed the microphone I
was wearing.

Do you have a happy place? I hope you do, no matter
your calling in life. If you don't have a happy place then
you've some work to do. Get started!

CHAPTER 6

BOOM!

"Nearly all the best things that came to me in life have been unexpected, unplanned by me." -Carl Sandburg

I'm going to share a fact with you because I have hit retirement age and can speak a bit more freely. For every person who can sing or play an instrument well, there are about 40 who think they can sing or play an instrument just well as. Here is another fact: No matter how hard a team works at planning an effective and meaningful Sunday worship service, something can and often will go wrong during that service.

When you combine those two facts you are ready to crawl into the next story. This is what I have learned.

Doris and Howard were convinced that they were great singers. They had forced themselves into singing a "special" on Sunday morning just before I was to preach. I will be honest with you and say I wasn't thrilled. A Sunday morning "special" in the day was a song that was sung immediately following communion service while the church offering was being collected. It was always called a "special" but was generally anything but. First, if it is a "special" is why one sung every Sunday morning? Second, let's be honest — the song is used to fill time when the offering plates are passed around. Maybe churches should be more honest and call this song the "Every Sunday Morning Time Filler Song." Also, to be honest, you must have a large number of people to have a quality subset of good singers. Before anyone misunderstands, I'm not saying that we shouldn't all strive to lift praises to God with what the scripture calls "joyful songs." (Psalm 100:2b)

What I am sharing is this: In most churches of smaller numbers, there aren't many quality singers. Most solos, duos, quartets and, dare I say "specials," are more like a Christian version of the old T.V. show "Amateur Hour." At best they become a holy version of karaoke.

This morning was different — and burned into the memories of many minds. This Sunday was a once in a lifetime for this preacher. As a matter of fact, I know of no other preacher or church that has ever experienced this.

You've met Doris and Howard. I want to introduce you to another group of people.

Over the years Jill and I became friends with a group of sisters roughly our age and their husbands. We all worshiped together. The sisters are Judy, Aleshia and Theresa. They all share the last name Kelley so they were known as the "Kelley girls." Judy at one time served as my secretary. They are married to Rick, Erik and John, respectively. We were all friends and shared several special days with the whole crew riding jet skis and enjoying cookouts. The guys and I played softball together, and John, Eric and another friend Harry and I traveled to NASCAR races together. We shared a worship home, interests and lives together. We have shared some interesting stories together. Little did Aleshia know what role she would to play in this morning's special

Back to the Sunday morning we're discussing. It was the 10 a.m. service and the worship area was full. We had enjoyed corporate worship in singing, shared together in the Lord's supper, received the offering and now was the crescendo leading up to the sermon — the "special!"

The husband and wife team had chosen an old song titled "Beulah Land." The song has never really made a lot of sense to me; it is about standing on a mountain and looking "across the sea, where mansions are prepared for me." It was written by a man named Edgar Stites and compares the post-civil war beauty of American landscape to heaven. Not exactly the most contemporary of Christian songs!

They stood to sing. The song featured the singing of a verse and then featured Doris on the refrain as she would sing, while holding the note for several counts, "Ohhhhhhhhhhhhhhh." Her singing of "Ohhhhhhhhh" was followed by her husband joining for a climatic hard "B." "Beulah land, sweet Beulah land, as on the highest mount I stand." Try to imagine it in your mind which won't be hard if you've ever heard the tune. "Ohhhhhhhhhhhhhhhhhhhhhhhhh BEULAH land, sweet

BEULAH land, as on the highest mount I stand."

As Doris sang, she had a bit of a nervous look on her face. She did a pretty good job really, but when she stood in front of a crowd, she had a bit of a deer in headlights look about her. Howard sang with tremendous amounts of vibrato no matter the song. They had gone through their dramatic rendition of the refrain as shared above, then the refrain again. After the third chorus they began the dramatic entrance into the refrain. Doris took a deep breath and reached high as she looked out over the congregation. "OHHHHHHHHHHHHH."

Then it happened. BOOM! A gun went off in the room. The whole auditorium of people levitated and fell back to their seats. I was on the front pew and my mind raced. I immediately looked at the choir, seated on the stage behind the singers, and saw a terrified look in all the faces. I especially keyed in on my wife's face and saw distress. Thoughts were racing. I jumped up, looked back and saw one man, a police officer, running out the back door to call for help and retrieve the weapon in his car. No one else was moving.

I then caught my friend Erik's eye. He was sitting next to Aleshia and was laughing uncontrollably. There was a puff of smoke in the air, and Aleshia looked horrified. Two other friends, Chip and James, were sitting in front of them looking terrified. Thank God it wasn't a gun!

What had happened? Months earlier, on January 2,

Aleshia left for a trip to the store. The night before, her children, along with some others, had been shooting fireworks in the yard. In the light of the day, she picked a few spent ones up and placed them in the garbage. In her yard she found an unspent firework. It was shaped like a champagne bottle, about four or so inches long and had a sting at the neck end of the bottle that you pull and BOOM! Confetti and a loud noise result.

Aleshia had placed this one in her pocketbook. Later that day she emptied the important contents of her pocketbook and stored it in her closet. A few months later, she carried it to church. She and Eric had brought their niece with them. She was fidgeting, and Aleshia reached into her pocketbook and gave the girl an explosive to play with. What could go wrong?

She held it up. Eric saw her and tried to stop it, but it was too late. She pulled the string! The explosion of fire, sound and confetti was right between Chip and James. James later confided to me that he thought he had been shot and wondered why it was not hurting.

Back to Doris and Howard. She was right in the crescendo of "Ohhhhhhhhhhhh" when the explosion took place. She never flinched and Howard joined in right on cue. "BEULAH land, sweet Beulah land." Sing it with me, "Ohhhhhhhhhhhhhh (BOOM) BEULAH land, sweet Beulah land, as on thy highest mount I stand."

I sat back down on the front pew, bowed my head and

began to laugh. My laughter signaled that all was OK! Doris and Howard didn't missed a beat, and the sermon began with a few investigative questions for Erik and Aleshia. There was a hearty laughter of relief by the deafened worshippers.

In today's world I am so thankful that's all it was. I am thankful for Doris and Howard, not the best of singers, but in love with Jesus. I am thankful for the many friends I have been blessed with and the roles they play in my life.

Now, a point to be made. I don't care what you have planned, it will rarely, if ever, go exactly as planned. Sometimes you need a plan B and sometimes you don't. So much of life just happens no matter the plan. The unplanned can be where the greatest moments of living are found. It is often in these accidents of time that we find, grace, hope, laughter, shared experiences and friendships that grow deeper.

I have changed a couple of names in this story, but not Erik and Aleshia's nor the rest of their family. I got permission from another sister, Sharon, my favorite of the Kelley sisters, to tell this with your full names.

Thank you God! I am thankful that I got to be there that Sunday. It is a Sunday I am convinced has only happened one time in all of Christianity, and I got to witness it!

"Ohhhhhhhhh, BEULAH land, sweet BEULAH land ..."

CHAPTER 7

Leadership

"A spiritual leader will first and foremost, have a calling from God. His work will not be his profession, but his calling." — Zac Poonen

I had often said that if I moved, I would stay in the Sun Belt, and I for sure wouldn't go back to Tennessee. I guess I didn't want to preach where I already had a reputation. Note to self, life doesn't always work the way we planned.

It was lunchtime and I had gone home to eat a sandwich, something I rarely did. The phone rang and I answered. The greeting was simple, "My name is Boge Dyer. (Boge is pronounced bow with a hard "g"). Do you want to come to Boones Creek?" The honest truth? I said, "What is a Boge?" We talked for 20 minutes or more. I still have, 20 years later, the paper I took notes on as we talked.

Roughly a year earlier, the then-president of Milligan College, Donald Jeanes, had given my name to the church as a potential candidate for ministry at Boones Creek Christian Church in Boones Creek, TN. In communication with President Jeanes, I had told him that

I wasn't interested in moving. I had filed the conversation away as a distant memory. Again, one wonders about all the "what ifs," but no more was said, and I had little thought about it until that call.

A minister had been there for 14 years and had moved to another church. Boones Creek Christian Church was healthy, had built a new building, and Boge shared that they wanted to grow. Was I interested? I agreed to meet with them when Jill and I were in the area on vacation. Interestingly enough, as things had changed over the past year, I would also be interviewing with First Christian Church in Johnson City, Tennessee, where President Jeanes was part of the search team. I really didn't think much would come of either interview.

The night of the interview at Boones Creek, I apologized to Jill for scheduling the conversation. I wasn't going to move back this close to home, and I felt that what I had agreed to was unfair to all. Nevertheless, Jill and I went to meet the leadership of the church. I'll never forget that night. We got there a few minutes early and met a couple of the leaders as the others rolled in.

Boge was there; joining the meeting as the last to arrive was Bubba. Bubba came into the meeting with denim overalls and muddy shoes. He is a dairy farmer and he 150% looked the part. I met a few others over the next few weeks of interviews and a visit to the campus. More about Bubba in a couple of pages.

Along with Boge and Bubba, I met Tater and Rabbit. Later, I met Tater's little brother Spud and a man called Monk. Believe me when I tell you that there were no Boges, Bubbas, Taters, Rabbits, Spuds or Monks at the space center.

The interview blew me away. These leaders flat loved the church and wanted more than anything what would be best for it. We talked for a couple of hours. When we were done the leaders stood and said, "When we pray at Boones Creek, we hold hands." We formed a circle, held hands and prayed for God's will.

Jill and I headed home and as we neared the interstate less than two-tenths of a mile away, I asked Jill what she thought. I told her that I was shocked by my sudden change of heart about moving, but if they were interested then I was too. She agreed. We drove in silence.

I visited the church building with Sam, one of the leaders, a couple of days later. I met several people during the visit, but I remember one in particular. Her name was Beth. She smiled and said, "You may be the minister we have been praying about for a year." I was blown away.

I returned to East Tennessee with some friends a couple of months later for an annual trip to watch the NASCAR race at Bristol Motor Speedway. Hey, I'm from the south. As part of the visit, I stayed a couple of days extra and, unbeknownst to my traveling buddies, I preached at Boones Creek Christian Church. Afterward,

I was voted on by the congregation as minister. I left immediately to return to Florida. I was driving a small truck and towing my Jet Ski. My friends and I had attended the race and spent the week on a lake.

I was at a welcome station in South Carolina taking a nap on the Jet Ski when I got the call about the congregation's vote. Our life was changing, and we would be moving back to Tennessee. What a scary time lay ahead.

I want you to take another inventory. This one involves some introspection. Are you happy where you are now? What needs to change? I hate change and it always takes me a few months to grow comfortable with it, but I have realized one very important thing. Change never asks if a person is ready! When we spend our lives trying to stop change, we are like a man standing on the shoreline trying to hold back the tides with a piece of plywood. You'll be knocked down and washed over. We were comfortable in Florida, but now was time for a change.

The hardest part of the move was our son Paul. He was born in 1985 in Florida — a native "cracker" as they would say. Paul had a great many friends and was playing high school football at Astronaut High School. If I may name drop, that school that produced NFL greats Cris Collinsworth and Wilber Marshall. Life for Paul was good. For someone that age, rooted and with friends, it can be a very difficult time to move. We had to talk.

The talk didn't go very well. There were tears and when I told him about the opportunity, he didn't see it as such. I tried to share with him a philosophy I adopted years earlier before our move to Florida: "We sometimes have to go to grow." He didn't see it that way. There was a long sleepless night and the next morning Paul said to us, "I've thought about it and if we need to move, I'm glad it will be to Tennessee. I already know some people there." Those words from our son screamed to me, "God is in this thing." Thank you to my son Paul for confirming God's will. As I said earlier, Jill moves well and loves the folks wherever she is. We were heading back to the mountains.

Paul marches to the beat of a different drummer. He always has, and I'm proud of him for that. He is a graduate of Johnson University with a degree in youth ministry and preaching. He serves as the director of a mission in Haiti. He travels to Haiti often and is in daily contact with the work. The Christian ministry is AHBZ, or House of Hope, and it operates a girls home, school and church in Port-au-Prince, Haiti. He has been involved with the work since 2010. He met his wife Kate through the work there and they are the parents of precious Amelie and our grandson Miles. They live in Savannah, Georgia, and Kate, a wonderful Christian lady, works for a church there. I'm crazy over Amelie. She is the world's greatest granddaughter and has me wrapped around her finger. Miles is my youngest grandchild. I call him miracle Miles because he was born early, weighed less than two pounds and was a little over nine inches long. He spent his first nearly three months on this earth in the NICU. He is now a thriving, active and handsome 18-month-old. Paul and Kate are tremendous parents. We are blessed!

Now, back to Bubba. His real name is David, but everyone knows him as Bubba, the name given to him by his oldest grandchild. One evening we were in a meeting where there was some passionate discussion about an important decision for the future of the church. There was no anger, but there were passionate feelings that ran counter to each other. Finally, it came down to a vote. What would the decision be? While the leadership operated on consensus, each man had to state a yes or no. The vote was four to three. Bubba was one of the three. After the meeting one of the leaders who was part of the majority approached Bubba. The man said softly, "Bubba, I'm sorry." Bubba looked at him and asked, "What are you sorry about?" "I'm sorry you lost that vote." I'll never forget what Bubba said! He looked the man straight in the eye, smiled and said, "I didn't lose any vote." He pointed to the exit and added, "When we go out that door it is seven zero, unanimous."

I observed a great leader at work that night. He was living the fact that when working with other people it isn't about winning and losing but about being together. I'm proud to have worked with Bubba. I have been blessed to work with many great leaders — yes, some better than others — but I'll tell you something very important. The best leaders love God and love people! I think the greatest leaders understand that the two go together in that order, and you can't say you love God without really loving other people.

I want you to digest this next thing I've learned from watching good leaders. Good leaders will live the reality that you don't have to like everybody, but you darn sure better love them. Take the time to ponder that for a bit.

I have learned a lot over the years about leadership and am the first to admit that I have failed miserably at being the leader that I wish I could be. I want to share with you a few of things that I have learned.

First, leaders must be trained to be good leaders. I want you to think about something for a minute. The apostles, who were handpicked by Christ, were not unleashed on the world until they had spent a three-year intern program with Jesus. Three years with the Son of God before they were unleashed to lead and shepherd the church. How many good candidates for leadership have been crushed by the weight of leading the church and have brought havoc into the church simply because they didn't understand biblical leadership? If Peter and John had to spend three years with Jesus himself, who on earth do we think we are to just randomly pick a name because of family ties or friendship and say to them,

'You're ready to lead?' Most church leaders are picked without a very real understanding of what it means to be a Spirit-filled leader. When the first leaders of the church were unleashed, they were men who had been with Jesus and were gifted by Jesus with God living in them through the Holy Spirit. That's pretty heady stuff that needs to be examined by all involved in choosing and being leaders.

I promise you that whoever you place in leadership has received some training, but rarely is it biblical. Many are trained by working under a difficult manager. Large numbers are taught that leadership is looking at profit margins or production numbers. Some are trained that leadership is loud and bossy. I've been made miserable by leaders who understood that their job was keeping an eye on others to find their failures. Few have been trained that leadership is to be like Christ. Godly leaders must be trained!

Second, and I think that this is very important, not everyone is called to be a leader. It is not a sin to not be a leader, but it sure can be a sin to accept leadership if you aren't ready to do so in a Christ-like manner. True and really gifted leaders are a rare breed, and you will never identify one by looking at their outside and their credentials. You know the best way to see who the real leader is? Look at who the people in the church are following and who are growing spiritually. Often the person with the title is not doing the leading. Great leaders in the corporate arena are not guaranteed to be great leaders in the church. The corporate world doesn't say anything about "So the last will be first, and the first will be last." (John 20:16) Jesus sure did. He also alluded to the fact that we must die to self.

Third, it is hard to be a leader, but it is real easy to take potshots. Over the years I have watched true leaders struggle to discern and do what they think is right. Sometimes the decisions being faced are fraught with possible failure no matter which way you go. Every time I've seen a decision like this reached there has been a handful tell anyone who will listen what is wrong with that decision. If you are a leader, don't listen to those folks. You know who they are! If you don't, just give yourself some time and you'll figure them out. A word of warning to leaders. You will be surprised and emotionally wounded by those who will take shots at you. Listen, I know this is an old piece of advice, but the potshots say more about the shooter than they do about the leader. If you have gained all the facts you can and sought God's will in humble prayer then make a decision and duck! The shots are coming and they won't be as bad as you think. The church needs good leaders, not good coddlers!

Another thing I've learned is that a church can handle about anything if the leadership is solid. First and foremost, the leadership must be grounded in love for God, the people and for the institution. The three go hand-in-hand. The church belongs to God and is made up of God's people. Leadership must also be united and act as one. There will be folks who will try to undo the work of the church or, I think worse yet, stand in the way of God's work being done. You'll always have folks who prefer new furniture over missions and mealtime over meal packs. Leaders must stay strong and united in taking the church forward. I've seen it both ways and, boy, united sure works better, and the men and women in the roles sleep better too!

Leaders never tear down other people. If a person is tearing down another person, no matter how failed the person may be, they are not leading! Good leaders seek to meet people where they are and work hard in love to bring them forward in Christ. There is not a person alive who doesn't have a lot of flaws that can be reason for gossip. A good leader will tell you why they should be loved. Solid leadership can take a mediocre situation and make it a victorious one. Weak leadership will snatch defeat right out of the mouth of victory every time.

You won't hear Godly leaders say things like, "he can never change," or "Her family has always been that way." Real leaders see all as children of God and will treat them accordingly. It is at God's discretion to exact vengeance and pass judgement and, like everything else, He will do a much better job. Godly leaders will often have their mouths shut but their hearts open.

Good leaders need good followers. We've all fallen prey to the false thinking that sees the leader as the one with power and the follower as the one without. I know churches, and I want to tell you something. Anywhere you find that philosophy of power among leaders you will find a stagnant or, more likely, a sick and dying church. There is nothing about healthy leadership wielding power. Leadership is about accepting major, high-pressure responsibility. All good leaders are followers somewhere in their lives and they understand the importance of following. Are you a good follower?

Maybe the most important thing that can be said about leaders is that they know how to love as Christ loved. If we will simply love others as Christ loved, then we will see tremendous growth among people. They will begin to leave behind fear and feelings of inadequacy. When people are loved they begin to smile and encourage others as they are being encouraged. When folk are loved they seek to help rather than attack those who are different. When followers are led by leaders who are feeding on the Word of God, they will begin to nourish themselves a bit differently too.

I hope you've noticed that I have not shared any difficult or painful stories about leaders. I could share some very difficult and agonizing leadership stories, but you know what? If I did, I wouldn't be much of a leader would I? Think about that and start training. The church is in a difficult world right now and we need Godly leaders who are willing to follow the words of the apostle Paul when he wrote, "Forgetting what is behind and straining toward what is ahead, I press on toward the goal to win the prize for which God has called me heavenward in Christ Jesus." (Philippians 3:13b-14).

This chapter closes with a simple scripture from the apostle to his younger protégé Timothy. Timothy had been entrusted with the organization of the church and the teaching of God's will among the men and women of Ephesus. The church there was in its infancy and had to do it right to survive. Paul began instruction and description of a church leader this way, "Now the overseer is to be above reproach ..." (I Timothy 3:2).

CHAPTER 8

Phrases

"Women are mean and men are stupid"
– My mother, Ethel Clark

My mother and I were traveling north. She had been to Florida to visit and, for the first and only time, the two of us were traveling alone from Florida to Tennessee. It was a pleasant trip on a pleasant day and we were driving through Jacksonville when mom asked me a probing mom question.

"David, is Billy having an affair?" My mother had gotten to know Billy through trips to Florida and visits to the church. I was taken aback by her boldness and framed my answer simply. "Mom," I sort of chuckled, "you know I can't answer that question and you also know that my refusal to answer means nothing." Mom commended me for not answering and then gave me a startling response. I'll share her response shortly.

My mother was widowed at age 48. She was young when my dad, a good man, passed suddenly. It was a terrible time for us all. I was only 17, my brother Kenneth was in Memphis attending medical school, and my oldest brother Robert was 26.

Mom had been working outside the home for a few years before my father's death. She worked as a deputy clerk in the court system and through her job would hear sordid details of a lot of divorces. I have often wondered what it must have been like to have lost someone you loved deeply as a spouse and had to hear others talk very despairingly about their mates.

You now understand a bit of her background and the hole she carried in her heart. You can grasp the despair she must have felt at hearing those who were married so willing to throw it all away. My mother had heard sordid details of affairs from men and women under oath. She shared with me a piece of wisdom. "David, I know you are trained in counseling and understand a lot about people, but I want to tell you something that's very true." I readied for a gem of knowledge. Mom said confidently, "Women are mean, and men are stupid!" Mic drop!

I may be exaggerating a bit, but I believe I drove at least halfway through Georgia speechless. My godly mother had just insulted every human being who has ever lived or lives. Here is the issue I was having. Remember, we are talking about affairs in particular. She was right! It seems that most every time I have dealt with this threat to marriage it has proven true. "Women are mean and men are stupid!" Thank you to my mom for that tidbit.

That is not the only phrase of wisdom I have picked up over the years. I hope the following things learned will serve you well in your pursuit of living as a Christian. I will share them in no particular order and I fully realize that you maybe have heard a couple of them before. If so I'm glad I can remind you.

I was pretty young in ministry when I first heard the next nugget I will share. To be honest I can't even remember who said it, but it was a passing statement made in a discussion I was a part of. I found it brilliant, and I have often pondered the phrase. Here it is: "What you win people with is what you win people to." Read that again and think about it for a minute. Since I can't remember who said it, you can attribute it to me.

I remember very early in ministry interacting with a church that had a softball team. The team was pretty good but not really good. The guys on the team took the whole thing pretty seriously. They were tired of being pretty good and wanted to do something to become really good. They did what any self-respecting church league sports team would do to up the ante. They recruited.

To recruit they had to overcome one slight obstacle. The church leadership had a requirement that if you played for the church you should attend the church. The leaders of the team had to figure a way to get around this because they had their eye on a couple of talents who weren't a part of the church.

Suddenly the athletes became evangelists. The invite to church went something like this: "We'd love to have you play softball with us. Would you be willing to attend church at least two Sunday mornings a month to play? All your fees will be paid for by the church." Now I'll admit that the invite was a bit more subtle than that, but you understand what I'm saying. The team became great!

Guess what happened when the softball league ended for the year? The fresh recruits stopped attending. True story? Yes! I've seen it more than once. What they were won with is what they were won to — softball.

Please don't pick on church sports. I played for years, loved every minute of it and saw it as a great tool for various reasons when treated right. Here is my point: How often do we win people to a style of music, youth trips, preacher personality, senior programs, self-help groups, special events or programs — only to see them walk away later? We witnessed them being won to everything but Christ and we never shared the love of Christ. It begs the question "What are we winning people to?" The simple statement as shared has really made me think over the years.

The phrase is simple, but I want to share with you how it has served me. That statement can be used as a standard for any idea that is floated or any sermon that is prepared. If you are a preacher reading this you know exactly what I mean. Are you using a fantastic joke or a warmhearted story as a major part of the sermon? I know humor is priceless and stories really illustrate, but you understand what I mean. Am I ultimately presenting the story of Jesus so people will be won to Him?

Leaders, what are you seeking to win people with? There is no program designed that should ever overshadow our ultimate goal of bringing men and women to a relationship with God. Remember, what you win people with is what you win people to.

My Sunday is not like most folk's Sunday. I must admit that what most would call a normal Sunday is not on my radar. Since I am the preacher that is, I assume, sort of a self-evident observation. As I write this, I am preaching three Sunday morning services and, on rare occasion, teaching a class. We also have a Monday evening worship. I love it!

Occasionally my Sunday routine changes, usually when Jill and I travel to visit our daughter in Florida. We always attend church there and get a taste of their normal schedule. Here is what I have found.

When we attend worship with them, I usually get up a bit ahead of everyone and ride a bicycle to McDonalds to eat breakfast and maybe read a bit for pleasure. Then I'll go back to their home, shower, change clothes and travel with them to their church. We will leave at 10:40ish to arrive just before 11 a.m. After the service, we'll visit, then go somewhere to eat. We're back at their house by 1:30 p.m. The afternoon will be a trip to the beach or a nap, maybe a swim or a bike ride, or one of the boys will have a soccer game.

I believe Christians worshipping is of overwhelming importance and yet find, as a participant and not the preacher, I am amazed at how little time actual corporate worship requires. The gathering is so important and yet requires so little of me. The process is so simple.

Recognizing how little it demands leads me to a simple observation. Why do so many who say they believe in God find every reason to not worship Him? Here are some of the reasons I have heard and then, much more importantly, some reasons I think are true.

People say, "It's the only day I have to sleep in." OK, is an 11 a.m. service that early? This one I hear a lot: "It is the only day I have to do yard or other work." Our church offers an 8:30 a.m. worship. There are churches everywhere that offer an early opportunity. In our community you could be home by 9:45 a.m. Here is a big one: "I'm so tired by Sunday. I have had to dress up all week for work. I just need a break." Well, where I preach we don't ask tired people to come and do marathon training. And have you been to church lately and seen the dress codes? Casual and comfortable is in.

I hope you get my point, but I bet you haven't. I'm not

trying to argue anyone into a Sunday worship gathering. What I do want to call your attention to are the real reasons I think a lot of people choose not to worship.

One of the most recent has been the recognition that the church has lost its way. It's very simple to observe when we take our blinders off. The scripture tells us we must show grace to all. The central character of our faith teaches that we should do unto others as we'd have them do unto us. Jesus also tells us that we are to love our neighbors as we love ourselves and, even radically, says that we are to love our enemies. He teaches us who our neighbors are by telling the story of a man crossing racial and socioeconomic lines. Read the story of the Good Samaritan told by Jesus himself. (Luke 10:25-37)

When I say the church has lost its way, I am speaking of the church as presented to the masses, the church that is observed in media, presented in academia and courted by politicians. It is the church that isn't about God's love but rather about dominance. It is the church that is known for a "we're right and you're wrong" attitude. The church that has lost its way is the one on display as an institution of self service and is inclusive of no one who is different.

I can state other reasons I believe people are using to not be a part of church. They have been hurt somewhere along the way by someone who attended a local church. They are angry for an issue of the past. Maybe they feel they don't fit in for whatever reason.

Please allow me in this chapter of phrases to share one I learned very early on that I believe is so very important. It is a very short phrase that is long on meaning: "Judge Jesus by Jesus!" Please, I beg, don't judge Jesus by me or by the men and women of the church. We are all struggling to follow Him and I assure you we are all failing at times. We're growing, but that's all we are doing. Please, "Judge Jesus by Jesus!" He loves everyone! Do not read that as a cliché. He loves everyone! That means if I have a problem with a person or a group of people I must change. Jesus is the standard bearer and the only true judge of anyone. That is why he told me and you that we shouldn't judge anyone. It make sense to me that I couldn't judge if I wanted to.

Well the same is true of us. Don't judge Jesus by the failings of those who are trying to follow Him. Judge Jesus by Jesus! If you are willing to do just that, well, you'll be in worship Sunday with the rest of us.

Here's another phrase. You'll like this one: "Turning a church is like turning a cruise ship, not like turning a canoe."

Allow me to introduce a story and my point. You won't enter a church that doesn't have some traditions in place. I guarantee you that every church has developed deep-rooted traditions that have stood the test of time. There are traditions that, from the outside, seem as quirky as quirky can be. A great many appear at best to be silly.

I want to share one such tradition and how silly it must have looked to all outsiders. This tradition is not part of my personal story. I could share several from my personal past, but names can only be changed so much. For that reason, I will share another.

There is a church in South Florida that, years ago, purchased an electric curtain that hung along the front of the baptistery. It was controlled from the back of the church and, when there was a baptism, it would be closed by flipping the switch. When the preacher and the candidate entered the water, it would open for the baptism. Oh, they were proud of the curtain and the modernity they had adopted. It gave them an air of sophistication. A tradition developed in the church.

As the service would begin, the organist would take her seat and play an old hymn on the Hammond. As she played, a man in the back would flip the switch right on cue. The closed curtain would open to reveal the well-lit painting of Christ's baptism on the back wall of the baptistery. The holy droning of the organ, accompanied by the holy reveal, was surely something that would impress the hardest of hearts who might wander into the gathering.

One Sunday the music began and the curtain opened right on cue. The congregants were shocked. Standing in the baptistery was a younger man with long hair and a beard covered in lather. It seems a hippie had entered the church because the doors were open, taken a bar of soap from the restroom and, undetected, found the enclosed baptistery and was bathing quietly. It was one of, if not the most, exciting Sundays the church had ever experienced. A long-haired Jesus and a long-haired hippie just hanging out together. The church ladies were shocked!

Now a serious question. What would you do to undo such a tradition? A tradition that had developed over years. It needs to be undone. Frankly, it just appears silly and will turn any new person off immediately as being outdated. Long-held traditions can often do that. What would you do?

Back to the cruise ship and canoe analogy. If I'm to turn a cruise ship I must have several things in place. Several people need to know it is going to be turned. If I'm going to turn it rapidly then valuable pieces of machinery must be made secure so that they won't fall overboard and the people on board must be out of harm's way. It can happen quickly, but there must also be proper understandings of the process and, for some, the whys should be known.

If I want to turn a canoe I simply stick the oar in the water and stroke hard once or twice. In the process, I may make someone fall out and may even capsize the canoe and lose any valuables in it.

I have seen a lot of young, newly-located ministers fail because they ignored and attempted to trample over long-held traditions. They were traditions that quite honestly had become, in a very real sense, holy to folks. You better not just grab the oar and yank. You'll capsize the whole thing! You must invest by listening and watching to see whom this tradition is important to. You must ask yourself, "Why do I want to lead to this change?" For all that is decent, be able to explain why it is important to change. Then you must lead, and understand that not everyone will go along, no matter how reasonable the need for change. You must love them no matter how much they frustrate.

Leaders, take a fresh look and see if there are any traditions that are in the way of reaching others for Christ. It can be hard to see things as an outsider might see them, but it can be done with a purposeful heart. Speak to each other about the needs and the whys and, by all means, remember that, "Turning the church is like turning a cruise ship and not like turning a canoe!" Make the changes that need to be made with a blend of boldness and gentleness, courage and meekness, strength and patience. Someday, I promise, it will be your tradition that needs to be changed. When that time comes display spiritual maturity by letting it happen.

CHAPTER 9

Ego

"You can either be a host to God or a hostage to your ego. It's your call." - Wayne Dyer

I was positive that anybody who saw me had a first and second wish. First wish was that they could be like me. By that I mean that they wanted to exude the look, the confidence and the manliness that I so easily carried. The second wish was simple. If they couldn't be like me they would at least want to meet me. Let me explain.

I had dressed in all black. Black boots, black jeans with a black pullover shirt and black leather jacket. I had on a black, full-face helmet with a dark, tinted face shield. Attached around the bottom of the helmet and tucked into the jacket was a quilted, black piece of material to protect my neck from cold weather. And, of course, I had black gloves.

The motorcycle was a black, 1000cc Kawasaki that had been bored out to a larger size that had a four-into-one header with a straight pipe. If that doesn't make sense, this will. It was loud and it would fly!

Do you get the picture in your mind? I didn't just look the part, I was the part. I was the epitome of "with it." I was Darth Vader before there was a Darth Vader. I was the leading man in a play called life. I was No. 1 on the charts, a rock and roll movie star for all to see.

I climbed on the bike and sped off to the graduate school library to grab a book I needed. It was late in the day and I arrived at the library as a lot of late-day classes were letting out. Several students were there as I pulled up to the front door. I was going to run in and right back out, so I parked by the curb in a pickup area. I thought that their seeing me would encourage them to continue trying to become as cool as I was.

I gave the bike an obligatory burp as I shut the motor off. I exited to the right side and kicked the stand down on the left. I had practiced that move. I would drop the bike onto the kickstand to the left as I turned my back to the bike to walk away. It seriously is a cool move to see. I only made one minor mistake. I missed the kickstand with my left foot and, with eight or 10 witnesses, the bike fell on its left side. I looked stupid! I dressed to impress an audience. I arrived in a loud mode to draw the attention of the audience, and I had an audience. Now I looked stupid.

I praise God to this day for the blacked-out helmet; I knew several of the men and women there from previous classes. I was isolated in my outfit but very embarrassed.

As I said, I looked stupid!

No one offered to help. Several were snickering and I was left to walk up a bike that weighed over 500 pounds. I did it. Adrenaline is a magic chemical. I carefully climbed back on the bike and rode away without the book.

Flash forward 40-plus years. I was still riding a motorcycle, but more mature and a lot more humble. Three of us were at lunch and I was telling the story on myself to a Christian brother named Mike and a longtime friend named John. John began to laugh and simply exclaimed, "That was you!" Oh my. Mike nearly wet his pants laughing!

One of the most amazing gifts we can have is an ego that is marked by humility and self- confidence. One without the other gets us in trouble every time!

Humility without self-confidence and we tend to spend our lives fearful of trying anything. We quickly become cowardly toward life. We cross a dangerous line and think that we are worthless and that all others have the moral and intellectual gifts to do and accomplish.

Self-confidence without humility and we will grow into arrogant tyrants. We will devolve to see others as beneath us and in our way. At worst we will see our fellow travelers as men and women to be used for our ends.

I really believe it is OK to examine Christianity and ask, "What is in it for me?" I say that because I find that we often present Christianity as some sort of a lose-it-all faith

where we are assigned to live a life of boredom and fear.
It is presented as a life without laughter and without joy.
The opposite is true!

What is in it for me? What does it mean to be granted
what Christ describes as to "have life, and have it to the
full?" (John 10:10). In my life it has meant a self-confidence
that has allowed me to step out and trust that it is
acceptable to try new things and meet new people. The
faith I received through Christ demanded that I step out
and try -- no matter how fearful I was. Boy, have I been
blessed! More about the blessings in the next chapter.

Most importantly, it means I have been gifted by God
for success in where he leads me. I have made many
mistakes and I have learned quickly how to laugh at
myself and to laugh with others. It means I will not be so
caught up in being right about everything, and that I have
learned to love life.

I want to share something with you. In my youth I
was sure that everyone wanted to be like me on that
motorcycle. In my spiritual growth, here is how I would
change the story. When I dropped the bike I should have
taken the helmet off, taken a bow and laughed really
hard at myself. For a few moments on that faithful day,
several students were given a reprieve from the stresses
of life and could laugh. I was the only one too blind to
see it. I missed out on the abundance of life we can
have in Christ.

Is there a dream God has placed in your heart that you need to try to make a reality? Go for it! Do you have a bunch of critics in your life telling you to always be safe? I bet they've accomplished very little. Ignore them! I sure wish I had ignored some dream killers in my own life. Do you have some Christian brothers or sisters you can share your dreams with and ask them to pray for clarity? Go to them right now.

Are you a Christian? Paul in the scripture wasn't -- and then he was. It was after he became a Christian that Paul said, "I can do all this through him who gives me strength." (Philippians 4:13) Life is hard at times for everyone. Only we Christians can still enjoy it.

One last question. If Jesus were alive today do you think he'd ride a motorcycle? I think he'd ride a Goldwing.

CHAPTER 10

The Other Side

"I have learned that most people rarely give a thought to being ready for death." – David Clark

It was 2 a.m. and I received the call with an address of where to report. I was the chaplain for the city of Titusville, Florida, police department, and there had been a single-car accident with a fatality. I would go to the scene and, after some preliminary tasks, would travel with an officer to deliver a death notice to the family. This night the notice would be given to a mom and dad.

This was not the first time I had carried out this task. I'm not sure how to say what I am going to tell you next, but I found the job meaningful. I would deliver to a family perhaps the worst news they would ever hear, and I wanted to do it with as much tenderness as possible. Believe me when I say that there is no good way to break this type of news. When someone comes to your door in a police uniform in the middle of the night it is never to bring good news. Tears often flowed before I said a word. I did the best I could to deliver the news quickly but with compassion. Being at the door meant that the issue could not be preceded by small talk. You've lost a loved one in a tragic way. I was witness to someone's world collapsing. As the bearer of news of this type I have been cursed, hit, and even one time blamed. I understand those feelings and those reactions. On a couple of occasions I found myself preaching the funeral a few days later.

I would break the news and offer to stay with them until other family members or friends came to offer comfort. I answered questions as best I could and offered to make any phone calls. I offered to pray with them. This particular night was especially troubling.

The scene of this accident was odd. The car was on an empty, major street in town. It was, as I said, late. The car had taken a sharp turn to the right and was resting with its front center against a power pole. There was very little damage. The car was still running when the first officer arrived, and the occupant was pronounced dead at the scene. An investigation began immediately.

The officers were very thorough, and it wasn't long until the plausible theory was floated that it wasn't a car accident but something else that had led to the death.

I remember the man in the car was young, handsome and lying across the front seat of the car with his eyes open, staring forward in death. There were no visible signs of injury.

After pictures were taken an officer rolled the body a few inches and retrieved a billfold for identification. The wait for the coroner began. No reason for hurry at this point.

The coroner arrived and, after initial examination, left with the body. A few hours later the news came. There was a small-caliber bullet wound in the right armpit with powder burn residue on the hand. The young man had been murdered! After he was shot his car had rolled forward a few yards until it hit the pole. The death had been quick as the bullet had penetrated his heart.

It turned out to be a drug deal gone badly! An arrest was made the next day; another young man and two families faced the unthinkable. It was horrible! That night will remain real and personal until I pass away.

I have, over the years, preached at hundreds of funerals. As you can surmise from this story there have been victims of murder and others who were suicides. There have been cancer deaths, heart attacks, strokes and various accidents. Many have been men and women who simply succumbed to old age. Tragically, a few were children.

With each, I have been changed a bit. Believe me when I tell you that being in a job that brings you up close and personal with death changes you in some very profound ways. Allow me to share a few of the ways.

First, you learn to truly hate death. As I have written, I have chosen my words carefully and I believe that it is of God that we hate death. We are, by our culture, blinded to death. We make it attractive; we avoid looking at it and talking about it. We oftentimes go away to some sterile environment to die. We protect our children from seeing it. We seem as a society to deny the obvious. We are all going to die!

Second, seeing the reality of death allows a person to really be free and driven to enjoy life. Someone who understands the promise of their own death will grab hold of every moment of life and seek to make it meaningful. Knowing that death will come, and can come, at any moment forces me to look forward even to the rainy days. Say it aloud to yourself right now. "I am going to die someday, and so today I choose to enjoy life."

I have learned that I don't want to spend my life watching other people live. It seems like we sure spend a lot of time sitting around watching other people live. We spend hundreds of dollars and countless hours watching other people do the living. Knowing that I will die has motivated me to work a job that matters and find hobbies that feed.

I have learned that most people rarely give a thought to being ready for death. That statement needs some explanation. Being prepared for death means living in such a way that when death comes, one doesn't have to fear it. Please hear me out on this one. I don't look forward to dying. I'm not crazy, but being ready means I don't have to fear the split second of death and what comes afterward.

Let's, for argument's sake, assume that the gospel is the truth. I believe it is, but let's all assume that it is. If I have a relationship with the creator of life and recognize how much he loves me then I needn't fear what comes next. As a matter of fact, I can look forward to the split seconds that are the first seeds of eternity that come immediately after death. Free from the fear of death I can enjoy life. Jesus said that he is preparing a place for me and I believe him.

I have nearly been killed on three occasions. Once, I was hit by a car while mowing my yard. That took talent on my part! You have to time it just perfect. While trying to act like a teenage at age 65, I nearly killed myself trying to ride a bicycle over jumps in the mountains. I look back on those experiences and there really wasn't a lot of fear but rather an "oh my" feeling. Yes, pain followed over the next few days and weeks, but the fear was shallow to nonexistent.

I know the pain of cancer or the gripping tightness in my chest is coming. Or, maybe it will be an instant where I realize an accident is happening. I don't know how it will come and I don't look forward to it. But, because of my faith in Jesus, I am going to embrace life until the end comes. I will continue to not take myself too seriously and spend as much time as possible enjoying being with others and hopefully bringing a little hope to their lives. I hope I never am guilty of robbing others of their joy; I ask forgiveness if I have. Mostly I am thankful for Christ who has allowed me to "have life and have it more abundantly." (John 10:10)

CHAPTER 11

Insert Title Here

"You know what they always say, 'You can't spell funeral without fun.'" – Author unknown

I estimate that I have led somewhere between 500 and 600 funerals. Each was unique. I have learned firsthand that sorrow is a major part of the human experience.

Funerals for children are the saddest and hardest to do. There are few words of comfort to offer a grieving mother and father. On the opposite end of the spectrum, I have officiated funerals where a person, because of age, welcomes pardon from this life. I'm not speaking as if the elderly embrace death in a morbid way but rather in the glorious anticipation of life in the presence of God. There is a hope displayed at death by a true believer that is very visible and a blessing to witness.

I can tell you honestly that an entire book could be written about some of those funerals and the events that surrounded them. I am going to share with you a couple of highlights.

One of the most memorable funerals was very early in my ministry. The funeral was held at a large veterans cemetery in a cold rain. Picture the pallbearers and me standing under a tent against the flag-draped coffin. We were looking across the casket at the elderly widow and family all seated. Water was falling in sheets off the tent inches from our backs and from theirs. I spoke words of comfort from scripture and then offered a prayer for the family. Right after I said, "Amen," began a 21-gun salute.

At the crack of the first rifle volley, the gentleman standing next to me flinched and slipped into the grave, pulling the American flag off the casket as he went down. He disappeared from the family's sight! I was not sure what to do and, as a very young minister, felt somewhat responsible. I feared I had done something wrong. There I stood holding a Bible, and one of the members of our formation went down when the shots were fired. A couple of the other men retrieved the flag then retrieved the man whose backside was now covered in red clay mud. His whole lower half had disappeared into the grave, and he had begun an immediate struggle for freedom.

I looked across the casket and my eyes met the eyes of the widow. She looked at me and began to laugh uncontrollably. She was doubled over and about to fall out of her chair. Everyone under the tent was soon laughing and gasping for air. What good sports! It is to this day the only funeral I've ever officiated or been too that ended with uncontrollable laughter from all present. Well, everyone present was laughing except for the funeral home director. They are never allowed to laugh!

The next Sunday, following my typical, nerve-racked Saturday night, I preached the morning sermon. Following the service, as the men and women were leaving, I stood at the back door and, as was custom, shook everyone's hand. The gentleman who fell in the grave came out and took my hand. His name was Durward, and he spoke with intent. "Preacher, if you should preach my funeral don't let them shoot those guns over me!" He then added, "They nearly scared me to death." I can honestly say that I smile every time I recall that funeral.

I want to share with you a bit more detail about one particular funeral. Remember the title of this chapter? "Insert Title Here." Read on and you will have a title for the chapter.

Shirley was very sick and dying. She suffered from cancer that had spread and the end was near. Her husband alerted me that she would be dying soon and asked if I could come over. I immediately drove to their home. We had prayer as other members of the family arrived. She would not live much longer.

There were, as always, attempts at idle chat among different family members. They took turns entering her room to visit their mom, grandma and aunt and tell her goodbye. Food was brought by neighbors and friends, and much of the gathering was in the kitchen. It was all very normal for the situation.

An hour or so after I arrived she died. I called the funeral home for the family and they dispatched a couple of men to pick up the body. They have a somber job, and I have always been amazed at the respect shown by those who carry out this job. They arrive, not always knowing what to expect and will, with tremendous dignity, remove the body to be transported to the funeral home. It is always very emotional for a family to witness their loved one being taken from the home.

This family was one that I knew well enough to be certain that something unusual would happen. The family couldn't do normal! I wasn't yet privy to what or how it would happen, but I knew it would happen. The reality was that there would be drama! I didn't know which member would be the catalyst, but I knew there would be an event. I knew them well.

I offered my condolences and was preparing to leave so the family could be alone when the husband made a request. "Could you please stay here for a few minutes? I would like to speak with you." "Of course," I answered. That request made me sense — the drama could be just around the corner. We were early in the process of planning and executing a funeral and the plot was already thickening.

The family members followed his cue and, after some initial planning and conversation, left. He and I sat alone.

The husband shared a bit of what he wanted as part of the service. We discussed some possibilities of times. I told him I would speak with other family members to collect memories and thoughts of what should be said.

I will stray here a bit and share with you my philosophy in reference to funerals with three personal beliefs. First, I believe the funeral is for the living, especially for those who were closest to the deceased. I like to remind them of personal memories and shared stories so that, in them, they might find comfort. I try to address them personally during the service.

Second, I believe what is said at funeral must be kept brief. Funerals are not the time to go on and on about grief, pain and sorrow. The family and loved ones have been through enough, and to drag them though a diatribe of grief borders on cruelty.

Third, I believe that Jesus is the only hope of the world! At the same time, I don't believe Aunt Matilda's death is the time to blast people with threats of hell if they don't know Jesus like Aunt Matilda did. I have never, in all my years of ministry, met someone who came to Christ because of funeral threats. I sometimes wonder if the opposite might even be true following some of the sermons I've heard at funerals. Now, back to the story at hand.

Remember I said that Shirley's husband wanted to talk

to me privately? Here is important background for you to know. The man was a tightwad. If you look that word up you will find it means a somewhat mean and miserly person. Now, let me say it again. He was a tightwad!

He took me into his garage. His garage was a typical, older home work garage. Think about a lawnmower sitting in the corner, a few gas cans and yard tools. A small enough space saved to squeeze in a car and, on one side, a work bench. The work bench had a few hand tools scattered around along with an oily rag or two. There was a saw and a couple of hammers hanging on the wall. The odor was one of petrol, and it was very warm.

He pointed to a small plastic box several inches tall and roughly 5-by-5 inches square and said, "Right there she is." I didn't say a word because I was confused. I wondered a lot but didn't say a word. One thing was for sure, the drama was beginning!

The husband went on to explain that Shirley had an aunt who had died a few years earlier as an old maid. Shirley and the new widower had promised that they would make sure her ashes were buried back in her home state of Indiana. She hadn't been laid to rest yet because he was a tightwad. He had checked on the burial with the cemetery and the cost was $600 to open the grave. He wasn't going to pay that!

He had told his sick wife that he had taken care of

it. You know where I'm heading don't you? Well, keep reading; you only know partially.

His question to me was simple. "Is there any law that states that two people can't be buried in the same casket?" I kid you not! He had planned this whole thing and had, at this point, dragged me into his plan.

Well, I knew the answer. There is no such law, but I wasn't about to become an active part of what he was doing. Besides, the funeral home director was a good friend, and I thought he should have the privilege of dealing with this query.

I shared that I thought that he should ask my friend Heath. After all, Heath was the pro at dealing with these things. I offered to meet him at the funeral home and help with the planning. I wanted to be there to witness my good friend's reaction to the question. It was important that I be there for more than normal reasons.

I want you to spend a bit of time thinking about the whole scene. Shirley's corpse is not cold, and her husband is plotting how to save $600 by placing the dead aunt's ashes between her knees. He made it clear that no one else was to know about it. Tightwad? Fits doesn't it?

Now, if you can't find humor in my dilemma you can't find humor! I met him at the funeral home. Heath explained the whole funeral process, taking notes in reference to next of kin, educational level, work history, etc. He gathered everything he needed for the obituary.

We made plans for the time and the place of the service. Everything was moving along in a totally normal fashion, and then it was time for the question.

I explained to Heath that the husband had an inquiry. The new widower asked, "Is there a law against burying two people in the same casket?" He then shared all the details about why he was asking. I was sitting with my chair next to, but just a few inches behind, the questioner and smiled at Heath. He looked down to feign thinking but was doing all he could to avoid laughing. He then answered, "No, there is not." It was settled. The aunt's ashes could be placed in the casket and the mourning husband could save a few dollars. Heath later threatened me for smiling at him. I was proud of the fact that I almost made the funeral director laugh!

The widower went to his car, retrieved the box and handed it over to the funeral home director. The director privately placed it between the deceased's knees. If there is a public ceremony that celebrates the placing of one person's ashes in another person's coffin I wasn't included. I'm pretty sure there is no such ceremony.

As I said, I have preached a great many funerals, but this is the only one that was a two-for-one. I had to make sure to not say "they" instead of "her" and, to be honest, I had to guard against smiling at the wrong time. I knew a secret that would have made a few people mad and a lot of people snicker. They were buried together in Indiana.

Imagine their surprise at the resurrection!

Disclaimer: If you're wondering, no, it's not your family. The family later learned of the action because dad let it slip. They were a bit angry with him but got over it. They got real mad at me for a while! They felt I shouldn't have known if they didn't.

Remember my friend Clark Scott from chapter 3? Clark was describing ministry one time and described it this way: "Ministry is the only job in the world where a person can buy a new pair of shoes, get them out of the box in their office, put them on and think, 'Boy, these shoes are comfortable.' The minister will then sit and study with their new shoes on and suddenly smell a foul odor and look down at their new shoes and wonder to themselves, 'How did that chicken manure get on my shoes?'"

I answered a phone call many years ago and went to be with Shirley's family. I did nothing wrong and got chicken manure on my shoes. But, I was blessed with a story to tell.

Years later, I shared Shirley's story with my secretary Barbara, who was also a very dear friend. She was a very classy and proper older-than-me lady who took care of me. Barbara made me look good as a minister. I knew she would find the story from my younger ministry days somewhat humorous. I also shared with her that I wanted to write a book someday about events and personalities I have been blessed to be a part of and know.

I told Barbara several humorous and different things I had experienced with funerals. "What could I title a chapter about funerals?" I wondered aloud. Barbara thought a minute, and totally unlike Barbara, answered my question. Thank you to Barbara for the perfect title.

Well, you've read the chapter and the title as printed is "Insert Here." Go back to the beginning of the chapter now and insert Barbara's title: "Hauling Ashes!"

CHAPTER 12

I'm Rich

"Sometimes people come into your life for a moment, or a lifetime. It matters not the time they spent with you but how they impacted your life in that time."
- Author unknown

I was new at the church and we were having a dinner. I was busy meeting people when a man came up and gave me an envelope with several pages tightly folded in it. In a rather thick, what I thought was British, accent he asked me to read the letter and then meet with him. "Sure," I said. He then added, "I want you to read it so that you don't think I am crazy when we meet." I was intrigued but had to wait an hour-plus to read the letter. Curiosity was flowing freely through my veins.

The gentleman who gave me the 10-page letter was not British but Scottish. Don't ever let your ignorance get you in trouble on that one. As he would later tell me when I was humorously accusing him of being British, "We Scottish may be a wee people but we be proud." Throughout the rest of this story, read his quotes with your best Scottish accent.

Back to the letter. The gentleman was born during World War II and grew up extremely poor. His family lived in a crowded apartment and he liked to tell that one of his aunts used to say, "We can survive the German bombs, but this baby crying is going to be the death of us all."

Eddie grew up in Glasgow and, like the rest of his friends, he played in the streets in front of the flats where they lived. Soccer was the popular sport. Eddie realized he was different from the rest of the kids when the older boys picked him first when teams were being formed. Eddie was good but, by his own admission, he struggled with self-doubt. All the greats do.

Eddie ended up playing for East Stirlingshire where he was discovered by the Chelsea Football Club. Eddie became one of the fiercest of defenders and was chosen to play (capped) by his native Scotland 23 times. He had a tremendous career for Chelsea as a starter for 13 years and, to this day, is the only player to become manager of the club where he played. After his retirement from Chelsea, he moved to Tennessee to be manager of the Memphis Rogues.

While in Memphis, Eddie met and married his wife Linda, a corporate lawyer. She brought Eddie to East Tennessee and to church where we met.

"David," (remember the accent) am I the most famous Scotsman you know?" Eddie often asked. "Eddie," I would respond rather frustrated. "You are the only Scotsman I know." Frustrated? Yes, because he always asked, laughing, as I started my backswing on the golf course.

We grew close and I consider it an honor that I had the privilege of telling Eddie about Christ and baptizing him. I am flattered that for the last 20-plus years he has called me one of his "mates." He has shared often that he never dreamed one of his best friends would be a preacher. (Preacher must be read with his accent).

His name is Eddie McCreadie. Look him up on Wikipedia. We have countless memories together. He and Linda are great people who Jill and I love deeply. There is a point to telling you about him. Keep reading.

Several years later on a mission trip to Haiti I met a little boy. The little boy looked sad. He had a rather prominent scar just below his right eye that served as evidence that life for him had been hard. I've a picture of him that is one of my favorites but is also one of pain because I know the story.

The little boy attached himself to Jill and me. We hit it off even though there was a language barrier. The young boy truly lived in a hopeless environment. Jill and I made him smile a bit but could do little more.

We were in an area of Port-au-Prince, Haiti, called Cité Soleil. The name means city of the sun, but in reality is one of the darkest places on earth. It's run by brutal gangs and is a place of human trafficking and murder. While there, we were surrounded by little children. These children exist in what the United Nations calls the second poorest slum in the world. A more accurate description of the place to me would be to call it the front porch of hell. It is a place where human life exists in unimaginable misery.

During our visit we were protected by 12 to 15 Haitian men who served as escorts so we would not be robbed or worse. They kept us inside a circle and wouldn't allow us outside that circle for even a moment.

The little boy's name was Frankie. I often wonder what his life is like today. The Haiti he lived in then was bad, but now I fear he may no longer even be alive. I hope he is alive and doing as well as possible; however there is no way to find out. He would be in his late teens to early twenties now. I pray he has not been lost to trafficking or to a gang.

In Haiti, we were part of the establishment of a small church attended by around 200 people. I hope Frankie found some hope from that body of believers. I can only pray that I will see Frankie again someday in a much better place.

Follow me back to Boones Creek Christian Church to meet another man.

"Hi my name is David." "I know who you are," was the weekly reply. Never a name. When I asked for a name the man would change the subject and would go out the door. I brought in my secret weapon.

"Hi, I'm Jill, David's wife. And your name is?" "It's good

to meet you," was the response he gave her. No more.

Six months and many Sunday worship services later I met a visiting young couple at church named Fred and Angie. I got to know them over the weeks that followed and once, while riding together on a motorcycle trip to Grandfather Mountain in North Carolina, I was invited to come visit them in their home and share more about the church.

Fred and Angie lived in an apartment that sat on a large farm in the middle of horse stables. Fred worked the farm and took care of fences, mowing, horses and other chores. We had a great visit and as I readied to leave Angie's phone rang.

"George would like you to stop by the house if you can," Angie said as she hung up. I answered in the affirmative that I would, and wondered to myself, "Who is George?"

I stopped at the house on the farm and knocked on the door. A gentleman came to the door. Guess who? You're right. George, the man who wouldn't give me his name.

I entered the house and we went to the living room to visit. The house was rather large and the den area had a large two-sided fireplace. The room was tastefully decorated but had teal colors prominently displayed with the name Hornets above the fireplace on a large plaque. "Wow, you must really be a Hornets fan," I said. "Yes," he replied laughing, "I own them." His name is George Shinn and he founded and, at the time owned the Charlotte Hornets professional basketball team. You can't make it up.

George and his wife Meagan have become our good friends. Jill and I help our son Paul and his wife Kate oversee the House of Hope, and George has been very helpful to us over the years. His reluctance to share his name was like Eddie's letter. Let's get to know each other a bit first.

Let me tell you why I've shared these stories. I have met and become friends with a world-famous athlete. I met a multimillionaire who came up from poverty to live in a world I'll never be a part of. I met a young man in Haiti who is among the poorest in the world. I've met many more who could be part of this story, but the point is simple. I would have never met these people if it were not for Jesus.

My father worked in a textile plant and died when I was only 17. My mother worked in the county courthouse. I now live in the home I grew up in, and my life has been made rich by Christ.

I've been to India several times, to Haiti over 30 times and led prayer for an NBA game. I've met Carrie Underwood and her husband Mike Fisher; Olympic gold medalist Scott Hamilton; and I've walked in a tent city in a third-world country. I'm good friends with a former NBA team owner and have been in his home, on his jet and aboard his yacht. I have watched space shuttle launches with VIP passes and baptized believers in the muddy creeks of Tamil Nadu, India. I've been the speaker at a college baccalaureate service in the states, and I have been chased by Hindu extremists for preaching the gospel in India. I've seen an elephant in the wild and met Buzz Aldrin, the second man to walk on the moon.

I've stood next to a cobra den in rural India and led a communion service at the rim of the Grand Canyon. I've officiated a wedding in Alaska and preached a worship service in the Florida Keys. I've been a speaker at senior rallies and a counselor at youth camps. I've worked youth group car washes and preached to day workers in a tea plantation. I worked at a carnival and sold fireworks in a tent while attending graduate school. I've preached countless funerals and celebrated hundreds of weddings. I have lain awake many a night concerned for the church — but always in the end I've found peace and joy in the church.

Most of my life has been spent preparing and preaching a weekly sermon to men and women who graciously tolerated my foibles. I have had the privilege of hearing well over a thousand people confess their allegiance to Christ and have had the joy of baptizing them. I have baptized in several states and in one foreign country.

I am rich! My life has been blessed in ways that, when I was younger, I wouldn't have dreamed possible. I was a police chaplain, a university board member, a foundation president and a keynote speaker. I was nearly killed on a lawnmower, on a bicycle and in a river. I have lived near the ocean and waded many a mountain creek. I've been threatened and I've been lifted up.

Jill and I have many friends who are sources of encouragement to us. I think of Herman and Carl, two men now in their mid-90s. Another friend, Jerry, was police chief in Titusville when we first met; we have been friends since the late 1980s. Then there is Harry and Debbie, whom Jill and I have been close to since 1990. Add in Larry and Judy who have been our friends since my first ministry in 1976. Sylvia and her late husband Tommy welcomed us to Florida and took us under their wings like a big brother and sister when we were so young.

Jill and I have four other great friends — Mike, Karen, John, and Tammie that we have a continuous text thread where we share pictures, jokes and lighthearted insults that bring smiles to our faces. I have people in my life who are part of running conversations and nicknames of endearment that are tied to shared experiences.

Only because of the blood of Christ have I met literally

thousands of people and traveled to places I had only heard about as a child. I have been blessed. This next statement is true for us all. Everything you have that is good is from God. Realize that and if you are looking you will see God in every memory and in the memories yet to be made. He has showered us all with blessings. To use an old tried and true phrase — God is so good!

CHAPTER 13

Observations

"Everyone watches. We watch sports, we watch movies and we watch children play. But very few really observe and it is in observing that wisdom is gained."
– David Clark

One of the things I have noticed as I get older is that life teaches us a lot of lessons. Let me say that another way: If we are observant and a bit mindful we will learn a lot by simply observing life. It seems that life's truths present themselves daily, and I'd like to share a few I have learned:

1. Find a foreign mission and throw your talents into it.
2. Most people are good people.
3. If you work hard at something and master your craft others watching will think it easy.
4. We are never the smartest person in the room but, as a Christian, we have access to the smartest person.
5. Most folk have an agenda; mature Christians always have the same agenda.
6. Some ways of dying are worse than others, but there is no good way to die.

7. Understanding the process does not mean control of the outcome.

8. The more someone says or acts like they don't care the more they care.

9. The greatest memories are always inclusive of others.

10. When you feel like you are stuck and can find no solution say a prayer and take a nap.

11. Personal dreams are to be pursued but rarely shared.

12. Order from the menu to enjoy, never to impress.

13. Affairs never, ever work out.

14. You won't be the one who beats the system.

15. Eternity is a long time!

16. If God ever said, "You can hate three people," I know who my three would be.

17. God will never say you can hate three people.

18. I've never heard a church argument based on scripture.

19. Social media's tap root is in hell.

20. The elderly are the most fun to be around.

21. Obnoxious old people were obnoxious young people.

22. A nice evening drive with no real place to go solves a lot of problems.

23. Motorcycle rides are gifts from God.

24. Experiences are way more important than things.

25. Laziness is way overrated.
26. Naps are not laziness.
27. Being with friends is way more important than the event you go to together.
28. Living and dying are equal parts of the same journey.
29. If you love people, it's hard to be honest. If you don't love people, you won't be honest.
30. Learn to listen to stories.
31. Learn to tell stories.
32. Examine often who you are trying to impress.
33. Some people are duty bound to make others unhappy and treat is as a calling.
34. I don't care what you've done or been, you are forgiven.
35. A lot of preachers are lazy; to them it's a job.
36. A lot of preachers are hard workers; to them it's a calling.
37. A lot of what we pay for is paying to throw our lives away.
38. Bake cookies because you love -- not to be loved.
39. If someone loves your cookies it doesn't mean they love you.
40. The word Christian loses it meaning with an adjective or as an adjective. Christian stands alone!
41. Not everybody will like you.
42. You won't like everybody.

43. No matter my age I've a lot more things to learn.
44. Where there is smoke there is not always fire.
45. Some people would be against Jesus coming back.
46. Hard work doesn't automatically mean quality.
47. There's more to be thankful for than to fret over.
48. You don't need to be positive about the outcome to implement a new idea.
49. Church dinners often become cooking competitions.
50. Busy does not automatically equate to Godliness.
51. Few people realize that criticizing the church is criticism of Christ's bride.
52. No church has it all right.
53. Not all children are gifted.
54. Find a hobby – or two or three of them – and enjoy.
55. Riding a bike is more fun than hiking.
56. Wrecking a bike hurts worse than falling down while hiking.
57. If you go fishing make sure to throw them back.
58. Try game hunting with a camera.
59. Politics has no place in worship.
60. If you're going to laugh at your wife's new haircut go around the corner to do it.
61. Spend time with someone who is dying well and learn from them.
62. We mow way too much and way too often.

63. Hell's fury will be worse than a woman scorned.
64. Riding a stationary bike is way too realistic an analogy for so many lives.
65. Two pairs of pants and four shirts would get most of us through daily living.
66. Strive to be like children having fun.
67. Grandkids' sports are more fun to watch than pro sports.
68. Spend time with older kin.
69. Few hills are worth dying on.
70. No one really cares how old the earth is or isn't.
71. Old hymns were once upon a time contemporary.
72. Contemporary songs will become old too.
73. Meetings are the enemies of accomplishment.
74. Going to the dentist is as important as going to the doctor.
75. Lying works until you get caught, and you will get caught.
76. Apologetics is often the enemy of faith.
77. Seek to be well informed in at least one major subject.
78. Never set a standard of faith that is based on opinion.
79. Christian men and women will differ on many subjects.
80. It's OK to suck your thumb when you're 40 if it helps.

81. Video games make the mind mush.
82. Donuts are better than donut holes.
83. Set some goals to help the earth.
84. Electric-powered yard tools are better than gas-powered tools.
85. Find something that is worth getting angry over and do something positive about it.
86. God is not the author of death.
87. Sleep is a great use of some of our time.
88. Avoid 24-hour news at all cost. You'll stop thinking if you don't.
89. When scared take at least one more step and see if God is there.
90. It's OK to mourn past losses, but don't get stuck in them.
91. The scripture makes more real sense than anything you'll read.
92. Find the one thing that's for you, and hold on tight.
93. Don't roll your eyes at other's interests or tastes.
94. Pick a holiday and make it the holiday for you and yours. Our family's holiday is Thanksgiving.
95. Read the opposing view of things you've an opinion about.
96. Never discount another person's dreams.
97. Fathers are just as important as mothers to a child.

98. Some people want to be victims. It makes things easy for them.
99. You'll never lose a friend picking up after yourself.
100. Women are mean and men are stupid.

I hope a few of these observations will resonate with you. Maybe I can save you some time in having to learn them yourself, or maybe you can just roll your eyes (see #93). My main point in sharing these observations is that we have all learned a thing or two as we have traveled through life. Why not make a list yourself? Start with one or two and watch how it grows. You've learned a lot in your life. Now, with all of that said, I want to share the most important thing I have ever learned and know for a fact. God loves you and God loves me. He proved how much by sacrificing himself for us!

CHAPTER 14

Start Crawling

"If you can't fly then run, if you can't run then walk, if you can't walk then crawl, but whatever you do you have to keep moving forward." – Martin Luther King Jr.

I want you thank you for crawling into my story. I assume that this will be the only book you'll ever read that talks about nude beaches, funerals, fireworks and baptisms. Believe me when I tell you that I have just scratched the surface of experiences I have been blessed to have.

With that said, I want to issue to you a challenge. Discipline yourself to crawl into your own story. Put pen to paper and create a record of as many personal experiences as you can. Set aside a regular time and jot down just a line or two that will help you to remember the events that brought smiles and tears, joy and heartache. When you do you will realize how blessed a life you have had. You will be amazed how even the difficult times have made your life rich beyond belief. You will be glad you did, because as you relive memories you'll experience renewed joy, forgiveness and self-worth. You'll discover that your life has mattered and will look forward to your future. Pleasant memories revisited are a gift of life relived and enjoyed afresh.

Thank you for reading. Together, let's look forward to our futures.

David in the mountains

David and wife Jill

David and Jill with grand children,
Liam, Jackson, Amelie and Miles

Liam, Jackson, Amelie and Miles

Son Paul with wife Kate, Amelie and Miles

Daughter Kelly and son-in-law James

Brother Robert and David

Eddie McCreadie and wife Linda

**Mike and Karen Lewis, David and Jill,
Tammie and John Payne**

George Shinn and David

David with Frankie in Haiti

With son Paul in Haiti

Acknowledgments

As I bring this book to a close, I am filled with gratitude and a profound sense of appreciation. It is with a heart full of thanks that I acknowledge the wonderful congregations of the churches I have had the privilege to serve. Your unwavering support, your open hearts, and your willingness to 'crawl into the story' during my sermons and now within the pages of this book have been a source of inspiration and purpose throughout my ministry.

I am indebted to those who stood by me and provided their encouragement during the journey of writing this book. My heartfelt gratitude extends, in particular, to my beloved wife, Jill, whose unwavering faith in me and this project sustained me through its creation.

A special thanks goes out to the dedicated individuals who lent their expertise to bring this book to life, tirelessly working on its editing and proofreading- Carrie Gunning, Mike & Karen Lewis, Sharon Barger, Candace Tingle and Leigh Ann Laube. Your commitment to this endeavor has transformed it into a piece I am proud to share with the world.

This book is not just a reflection of my life in ministry but a testament to the collective spirit of support, encouragement, and faith that has guided me on this remarkable journey. To each and every one of you, congregants, supporters, and friends alike, I offer my deepest gratitude and heartfelt thanks. May this book continue to inspire and uplift those who 'crawl into the story' within its pages."

About the Author

David Clark is a 1976 graduate of Milligan University with a Bachelor of Arts in preaching and a 1983 graduate of East Tennessee State University with a Master of Education in counseling. He and his wife Jill have been married and have served together since 1976.

David enjoys sharing stories from his ministry and, in telling them, challenges others to stay firm in their faith. As you enjoy these stories, you will laugh, hopefully relive an emotion or two and be challenged to live and love your life more.

As you are drawn into David's story make sure to look at your own life. You have lived a great story as well and it is worth telling.

Made in the USA
Middletown, DE
29 September 2023

39774873R00080